NUMEROLOGY-ITS FACTS AND SECRETS

OTHER BOOKS
BY ARIEL YVON TAYLOR

NUMEROLOGY MADE PLAIN
THE SCIENCE OF NUMEROLOGY
FINDING YOURSELF BY NUMBERS

NUMEROLOGY
ITS FACTS
and
SECRETS

VOCATIONS
PERSONALITY KEYS

BY

ARIEL YVON TAYLOR

AND

H. WARREN HYER

SAGAR PUBLICATIONS
Ved Mansion, 72, Janpath
NEW DELHI-110001.

Printed in India 1973

Reprinted	*1989*
Reprint	1994
Reprinted	2002

Published by : N.K. SAGAR, for Sagar Publications New Delhi
Printed at: Gayatri Offset Press, Noida.

To THOSE WHO HAVE MADE THE DISCOVERY
That "All the world's a stage
And one man in his time plays many parts";
That each one has *many* talents,
In fact, has Ten from which to choose;
That in this rapidly changing world,
He who buries his Light in ONE task only,
Sooner or later "is cast into outer darkness, —

Uncovering the other Nine Talents,
Is the purpose and pastime of this little book.

* *

With a *Vocation* and a *Hobby*, if one *Knows how to Play*, he already has a triple start on the road to abundance.

When he puts so much joy in his work that his work becomes play, and so much energy in play that his play becomes a hobby, an avocation worth while, he establishes before he knows it, *three* avenues of income and expression in place of *one*. The other *seven* should follow naturally, as combinations of these three primary colors of the happy life—

VOCATION—AVOCATION—and the SPIRIT OF PLAY!

CONTENTS

PART I

Rhythm and Vocations

[7]

FOREWORD

*"All life is music
If you touch the note right
And in tune."*
—JOHN RUSKIN

MUSIC, in its Octave of Twelve notes, from which all music is written, reflects the rhythm of life itself, in the Twelve types of people born in the Twelve months of the year, giving us all the variations in human nature.

Yet like 1:00 A.M. and 1:00 P.M. on the clock, each note has its opposite pole for balance and harmony. When you meet another whose rhythm is the same as your own, he or she may be your "Balance-wheel" or "Challenge!"

Twenty-five years experience and research in the Vocational and Personnel field, choosing one with certain ability for a special activity, have brought proof beyond doubt that:

   a. Success comes more easily to one who is doing what his soul longs to do . . . and that this Inner Urge may be found in the *Date of Birth.*

   b. There are definite notes of harmony between a successful man and the Company which he serves, to be found in Name and Birthdate of both.

   c. The rhythm of nature reflected in Spring-Summer-Fall,—3 growing seasons of 3 months each, and the Winter arc of 3 to carry one over into the next Octave of growth, applies equally to man.

   d. As at 3, 6, 9, 12, the hands on the clock change their direction, so at the end of 3, 6, 9 or 12-year periods, a change of direction in one's activities should mark a forward swing into a new Season of greater expansion. growth, or harvest.

Here we can give only a glimpse of the basic nature of the Twelve "notes" in the scale of human nature. Each has his own "tone," which touched aright, brings forth a harmony response.

Toward this greater understanding of yourself and others, we trust that getting acquainted with the other Eleven types may prove a stimulating adventure in personal, social and business relations.

PART I

Invoking the Law of Rhythm to Bring Your Heart's Desire

Vocations and Avocations

Chapter 1

YOUR DIVINING ROD

THE SPIRIT OF PLAY

'Tis said that the quickest way to obtain your heart's desire is to *play that you have it, now!*

The spirit of play relaxes the mind. Your set plans or problems are, for the moment, set aside. In a happy unguarded moment, may come that idea which will turn the tide. Only thus, in a care-free mood, may the "magic rod" of Intuition uncover new sources of wealth for you.

"New wine, we pour not into old bottles," nor may we expect a fresh supply if the present vessel, full of old concepts and set formulas, remains carefully corked and guarded.

One must occasionally empty his mind of all concern over Past, Present, or Future, if he would receive a new influx of vim and vigor with which to truly attract his own.

Thus, in the spirit of the day, with the search for gold and buried treasure back in vogue, we will take our divining rod and join the prospectors in a search for hidden wealth in the realm of Human Nature. There, rich finds already made, disclose diamonds in the rough and gold mines of undiscovered talent.

In the hunt for buried treasure in the realm of Human Nature, your divining rod of Intuition plays a most important part Here, as in every other true sport or achievement, the pleasure of winning rests in that knowledge and application of technique which enable one to win over his opponent, or the situation, without undue stress or strain.

To divine or anticipate another's next move, or sense the cause of a silent mood, already gives you a point of advantage. When you can follow this step by step, by further agile penetration, you have learned indeed to wield your magic rod with agility.

"To divine," says Webster's dictionary, is "to perceive through reason, sympathy or intuition; to detect."

Reason, sympathy, and intense desire may open the way to many treasures, but unless to these be added Intuition, one is apt to miss the "great adventure," as did the man in Dr. Conwell's famous lecture, *Acres of Diamonds.* Having traveled the world over in search of wealth, he returned after many years, poor, footsore and weary, to find the greatest mine of his time in his own back yard.

That which is far away is always more alluring than that which is close at hand. But why travel to distant parts, when by use of your "magic rod" you may unearth rich treasure right where you are.

As recently as 1933, in a small town in Nevada, we are told that a group of unemployed, tearing down a shack for firewood, detected signs of ore in the rock beneath. They took a specimen to the assayer, who sent back for more. The owner was sought, and he, unaware of his *near* good fortune, sold for $150 a bonanza gold mine. He was an unemployed miner, familiar with ore in that locality, who had "never thought to examine the quartz rock on his own lot."

Everyone has some good hidden from view which may be brought to light by the divining rod of his Intuition, when he becomes relaxed and sufficiently poised to let the "rod" turn in his own mind and lead

[12]

him to the next step, instead of using his own will to force a situation and *make things come his way.*

When we go after a thing too strenuously, nine times out of ten we drive it from us. To receive, we must attract. To attract, we must be magnetic. To be magnetic, we must have a strong hidden force at our command which flows through us easily, smoothly, without any apparent effort of will. This requires a center of poise and balance. That is attained only when we can throw off our worries and stabilize ourselves with a new influx of power, allowing one part of our nature to rest and recuperate while we abandon ourselves to its opposite pole.

Chapter II

HAVE YOU A DEEP DESIRE

Of which your reason and sympathy approve? Then how may it be obtained?

Reason as far as you can. When you can go no farther, stop. Sleep over it. Be quiet, and *listen.* 'Tis then that Intuition speaks. "Intuition," Webster tells us, "is immediate apprehension; instinctive knowledge; ready insight"—an immediate knowing without benefit of books or other outside information.

With intuition, one is able to discern where undiscovered talent lies, whether the "gushing" of a new acquaintance be only surface deep with a dry well beneath, or a vague proposition holds any vein of merit.

Intuition is one of our highest faculties. The higher one goes, the larger his view, the more impersonal he becomes. He sees farther and thus notes many shortcomings in those who before seemed so necessary to his happiness. He becomes more willing to let go. It is only the child in understanding who grabs for everything within reach and insists on holding on. despite the danger, ill appearance or unwilling response to his demands.

When your desire reaches Up to include the best good of all, you tune in with that higher force of Intuition which sees farther than your conscious mind. Then, if you will deign to listen, a happy surprise may await you.

Do not expect the answer in loud, deep tones which all the world may hear, but in that quiet rhythmic response which first calls to mind something not thought of before (or long forgotten), perhaps an odor, tune, or a certain inflection of the voice, setting a whole train of thoughts in motion. Respond quickly before you lose the impression. After the singer on the radio has finished and you turn to another number, the rhythm of the former begins to fade away; so will the intuitive impressions you receive, if you do not act immediately, before another idea claims your attention.

BE DEFINITE

Know what you desire, then set its vibration in motion, right where you are. If you persist, you will, ere long, be drawing in its fulfillment as the fisherman does his line, filled with a rich catch, because you have used the proper bait.

Should you fail, despite the sincerity of your desire, remember that everyone is magnetic. You attract those experiences which strike a responsive note, somewhere in your nature. To seek outside the realm of possibilities for the fulfillment of your hopes is to court ultimate failure, but, knowing who and what you are, the extent and nature of your own power, you can place it where it will count for the most.

One does not seek deep water fish in shallow pools. The experienced fisherman with hook and line goes *where* and *when* his catch is apt to be most abundant and, knowing the instinctive desire of fish for food, provides the bait that is most alluring.

Immediate response in any realm comes from meeting that desire which is uppermost in the nature. But remember, Intuition works both ways. You may be able to "put one over" upon the consciousness of the fish, but with those who have an awakened mind and higher instinct, an insincere motive registers immediately upon their sensitive nature, bringing a reflex of rebuff, silence, or an uncomfortable, cold atmosphere.

Therefore, *keep your motive clear* and, with sincerity of purpose, exercise your reason. Observe the nature or desire of that person or thing which you wish to add to your present good. Then setting in motion the particular rhythm which characterizes its nature, you may invoke your "magic rod" of Intuition to reveal the next best step.

[15]

of thoughts in motion. Respond quickly before you lose the impression. After the singer, or the radio has finished and you turn to another number, the rhythm of the former begins to fade away: it will the intuitive impressions you receive, if you do not act immediately, before another idea claims your attention.

Chapter III

RHYTHM

"Rhythm is a regular recurrence of accent, heavy or light, in stated periods of time." Where you place the accent determines your progress in the harmony of life and differentiates the results obtained.

Regular recurrence *in stated periods of time* makes Time, the great recorder, a factor to be reckoned with in any event, small or great. Time can be measured only in terms of Number. Of numbers we have only Nine, without which there would be no rhythmic hours of work or play, no money to count, no taxes to pay. . . .

But, if there be "a number of things" which you feel would add to your comfort or pleasure, there is no reason why you cannot prepare to enjoy them now.

Every phase of life has its own variation. As the pulse, the breath, the swing of the pendulum to and fro, register a certain number of movements per minute, so does everything with a specific identity reflect this universal breathing in and out, in rhythmic cycles of time.

In rhythm with the waltz, the dance brings joy and pleasure, rejuvenation and youth. Out of rhythm, you are out-classed, and soon become a wall flower. The definite swing of the 4/4 march-time tread arouses the spirit of patriotism, whether it be soldiers going to war, or the winning college band. The more you observe the rhythmic sway of the world in which you move, the more magnetism at your command.

RHYTHMIC REPETITION DEVELOPS THE INTUITION

Any method of reasoning based on *Number*, followed consistently for an extended period, develops the Intui-

[16]

tion, particularly in that line where the thought has been centered.

Why? Because the regular recurrence of accent, accompanied by the same thought, develops a well-rounded brain cell, able to hold within itself the essence of such knowledge. Ever after, it is instant in response when an energy wave of like rhythm comes in contact with it.

RHYTHM ESTABLISHES HABIT

Professor James, eminent psychologist, makes the statement that "any act or thought repeated consecutively for forty-five times without failure, becomes habit."

Habit makes for Immediate Knowing without stopping to reason things out. When anything becomes "second nature" one no longer needs to weigh, measure, or read the printed directions.

The man who each day measures three pounds of grapes for a quarter soon guesses the weight at the first try. Those who make the final estimates of cost or time in any realm, owe their success to that intuitive knowledge which comes from repeated effort.

The woman who learns to cook scientifically, who carefully computes each ingredient, finds eventually, as do all others who faithfully work with Number, that she can estimate the correct amount without stopping to measure. When this point is reached her Intuition is developed in that particular field. This is no assurance, however, that her intuitive judgment is equally good in understanding and handling Sam, Henry, Mary or Jane, and in bringing them over to her way of thinking.

However, this is not such a difficult or impossible task when one remembers that everyone is running true to form, according to the law of his own inner nature. That nature, when understood, will be seen to be but the reflection of the particular rhythm with which his being is in tune.

As all forms of energy yield a harmonious response when a kindred rhythm is met, so may you, by discerning the innate nature of another, apply those stimuli which will awaken a happy response and make for harmony in your realm.

[17]

Whether your present query be WHO? WHAT? WHEN? WHERE? or WHY? you may, by the *Rhythm of Number,* invoke the aid of your "magic rod" and behold your doubts resolve in wonder.

Chapter IV

THE WAY OUT!

0—1—2—3—4

Every Number has its opposite poles. What may seem ill or wrong to you may only be a good thing gone too far. Strive to re-establish the point of balance.

One day on the calendar is in reality half day and half night. So does every unit of energy have its dual aspect, that which it really is, and that which it seems to be.

This interplay of opposing forces, this attraction and repulsion, is what makes life worth living. Without the magnetic and electric interchange of sunshine and shadow, light and dark, heat and cold, ebb and flow, come and go, one would perish of monotony. With an understanding view of both sides, balance on one point leads to the next higher step. Thus may you balance your light with its shadow, and move forward into a new and larger experience.

In rhythm with wind or weather, you are prepared for both. With a knowledge of the energy waves about you, you may anticipate the next one, and jump the breakers with glee at the proper moment without being bowled over by waves of depression or caught in the undertow. Observing each wave as it comes and catching its rhythm, you may use it as a life-buoy to lift you up and over to the next higher view.

0

The Cipher represents the Universe or Seed which holds within itself all the possibilities of a complete cycle of growth. It has a rhythm invisible to the outside world.

Should you ever feel that you have been "reduced to nothing," remember, this is just the winter season before a new sprouting experience begins. The seed must fall to the ground; it must leave that to which it has been attached, and go through a period of apparent inactivity to the outside world before the time is ripe for it to burst forth into a new period of growth. Be still, and listen. Receptivity to a new idea may be your Way Out.

1

1 is staccato-like in action. 1 always stands alone, as the first in anything. It is the Idea, the Creative principle, generating the first movement of life. Positive and masculine in nature, 1 represents that decisive action which enables one to make a decision and step out into a new field.

The pioneer and inventor who has the nerve to blaze a trail for less adventurous souls does not wait for the approval of family, friends, or community. If he did, his identity would soon be lost, but if he keeps on "keeping on" he will eventually tune in with those who can provide the necessary environment for the healthy growth of his plan.

THE WAY OUT FOR ONE
WHO HAS 1 OR 10 IN NAME OR BIRTH

Those with 5 in Name or Birth also take notice. 5 and 1 have many attributes in common. Both love change, variety, freedom, and have the creative urge of the inventor.

Those with 7 in Name or Birth also take notice. 1 and 7 should both hold their own counsel, and "paddle their own canoes." Both must have the nerve to stand alone, with faith in themselves and their ideas.

Spell out your Name with Character Grams or number the alphabet as shown here:

a b c d e f g h i   j k l m n o p q r   s t u v w x y z
1 2 3 4 5 6 7 8 9   1 2 3 4 5 6 7 8 9   1 2 3 4 5 6 7 8

Add letter values of each name. Then add totals for final number. *Birthpath* is number of month, day and year and their final total. Reduce the year and all higher numbers by adding their digits: $1 + 9 + 3 + 4 = 1 + 7 = 8$. See examples in Chapter X.

*1 is a part of every number, hence everyone should heed the suggestions for those with 1 or 10 in name or birth. In some measure the same principle may apply to you.

The quickest Way Out for the *One* who has a *new idea* that he deems worth while is to keep his enthusiasm to himself and not confide his secret to another.

Ask not for assistance, advice, or sympathy, but be willing to cut loose from your moorings and make a dash for independence quietly, before others are aware of your venture. Then be willing to continue alone for two more steps until, in the third your plan becomes more clearly visible.

The century plant blooms but once in a hundred years and then has all the town crowding round. It has kept so still for a long time previous that no one would dream of its ultimate beauty of bloom. The same policy would be a wise one for any 1 who desires to put a new idea over upon a credulous or doubting public.

When a 1 becomes lazy or, as a dreamer, procrastinates, he is soon absorbed by stronger notes around him, and his dream, for the present cycle is lost. He must await another lull before his voice may again be heard.

THE RHYTHM OF 2

Every tone has its echo, every tide its ebb and flow. Everything on which the light shines, casts a shadow. 2 in *action* and *reaction*, is the rhythm of Two beats to a

[21]

measure, as Day and Night in equal swing give us One day of time.

2 as the balance between opposite poles, the beginning and end, inside and outside, top and bottom, there and back, *is the law of duality*, reflected in the principle of give and take, cooperation, and the blending of opposing views into a common interest.

Since "it was not good for Man (1) to live alone," Woman (2) came into being to reflect the feminine qualities in Man, he in turn, reflecting the masculine side of her inner nature. So do we need each other.

But unless two people closely associated have a center pole of interest, their paths are apt to fall apart for lack of something to hold them together. Or, if one sets up his will against the other or through negativity refuses to play his full part, separation and dissolution are bound to occur.

2, being made up of 1 and 1, sees both sides of any situation. He can tear things apart so easily, and so quickly discern the lack of balance in any person or thing, that he may easily fall into an unpleasantly critical attitude. The nagging individual rings his own death knell by continually calling attention to the other's shortcomings. He should cease to analyze unless at the same time he can offer a constructive remedy in a genial, jovial frame of mind.

A Negative 2 wants peace at any price, he becomes too servile. Oftentimes those for whom he has been too solicitous turn their attention to someone else whom they cannot dominate, because it affords a greater thrill.

THE WAY OUT FOR THOSE WITH 2 OR 20 IN NAME OR BIRTH

Those with 6 in Name or Birth, also take note, as 6 is 3 × 2.

Keep the atmosphere clear.

The rhythm of each number produces its own distinctive atmosphere. It includes all that have gone before, and one more. Sometimes it pays to play on the key of the one below until you have his or her undivided attention.

The *wise* and *alert* 2 uses his wits and tact to observe

the chief desire of those about him, then introduces a new note of color along such line and gains their hearty cooperation.

In 2 we have the qualities of 1 and 2 producing 3. 3 has a sense of humor, he refuses to take life too seriously. Reaching out for the positive aspects of 3, 2 leaves his own plane of duality behind and learns to enjoy life in a happier vein.

He should make it a game with himself to find something in the other person to commend, even if it be a difficult task. Thus will he attract that reflex of good-will which is so essential to his happiness and well-being. As a constructive analyst, he should have no peer. An organizer of system and detail for others, he should do as well for himself, and make every moment count toward his own higher good.

THE RHYTHM OF 3

Youth and *Happiness* are reflected in the waltz time rhythm of 3.

3 as a blend of 1 and 2 in a joyous expression of life, represents the child, who, as a new center of interest, changes the accent of the home from father (1), or mother (2) to that of his own, the third person of the family trinity. For the time being, the whole world revolves around him, and rightly so. There is a reason:

3 is the first number of completion. Every three numbers, following the creative 1, add to 9. 9 is the symbol of the world, or a complete cycle. In the circumference of every circle we have 360°. $3 + 6 + 0 = 9$.

All progress moves through cycles of 3 to completion in 9.

1, the motivating factor in every principle of growth, stands alone.

$$\frac{2 + 3 + 4}{9} \qquad \frac{5 + 6 + 7}{\frac{1 + 8}{9}} \qquad \frac{8 + 9 + 10}{\frac{2 + 7}{9}}$$

$$\frac{11 + 12 + 13}{\frac{3 + 6}{9}}$$

The childish 3, with the accent on the last measure, calling attention to himself, interested only in his own comfort and pleasure, sometimes never grows up. 'Tis then he follows the shape of the figure 3 in its two curves, his friends, money, and means of livelihood are apt to roll in and roll out. Too generous or sympathetic, he scatters his energies and his money, and is pulled by his friends first this way and then that.

Friendship is essential to the 3. In the social whirl 3 is in his glory, but going round in circles, even if he does rise on the social ladder, does not always bring that satisfaction which he seeks.

When 3 stops to take stock of himself, he pulls in his purse strings which, in the figure 3, are flying open, and exercising the initiative (1) of his father and the tact and analytical ability (2) of his mother, ties them behind his back and begins to place his thought and energy where they will count for the most.

Now, giving to each side of his nature, physical, mental and spiritual, its proper due, he becomes the triangle of Three equal sides whose reflection makes the Square, his next objective. Able to see the next step, though at present it is only a shadow, he begins to use his imagination to reach it more quickly.

Three is the picture-making faculty. The child's whole world is colored by his make-believe. For the older children of unnumbered years, the movies or a good story, provide that stimulus to the imagination which keeps them forever young. In rhythm with their profession, many of our famous motion picture stars have a name or birthdate of 3.

A combination of 1 and 2, 3 is the *Inventor* with an original idea (1) who gathers his material or people together (2) and sees his dream blossom (3) into reality, when he learns how to coordinate and center his Threefold nature. Edison affords a typical example. Adding the letters of his name, according to alphabetical table shown on a previous page, we find that the vowels total 20, the consonants 10, giving a final total of 30. In his surname, —indicative of innate talent and ability, is found the complete creative trinity of 1, 2, 3.

[24]

As nurse, artist, actor, doctor, food specialist, enter-tainer, or kindergarten guide, meeting every situation with a gleam of humor, 3 finds his success and joy in bringing joy to others in his world.

THE WAY OUT FOR THOSE WITH 3 IN NAME OR BIRTH

Those with 9 in Name or Birth, also take note, as 9 is 3×3.

Those with 6 in Name or Birth, also take note, as 6 is 2×3.

With his 3-sided nature, a 3 who has not centered his forces may at different times reflect sunshine, moonshine, or be the mere shadow of a more dominant mind. But he has 3 Ways Out of any present difficulty.

1—By exercising his imagination he may create the picture he desires and play that he has it *now*. Here he must be careful not to take two or more views on one film, as he will do if he changes his mind before the first idea has been developed. He must make a decision and hold it for a reasonable length of time.

2—Quieting the emotions, let his imagination dwell upon the idea long enough to build a clear picture. Then let intellect and reason weigh the pros and cons and add further details.

3—Completing the picture in every detail, with the accent always on the same spot, he sets up that rhythm which brings into play the "divining rod" of his Intuition.

With Intuition, Intellect and Imagination, all focused by the Will in the same direction, the picture gains clarity, capable of realization and the formulation of a definite plan in 4.

3 ATMOSPHERE

3 is $1 + 2 + 3 = 6$. 6 stands for expression through the voice. It gives an urge to talk. In one's enthusiasm over his new plan he may wish his friends to share it too. Not until the venture has reached the Sixth stage, however, is it safe to discuss it with others, and even then the important secrets should be left until a later date. Therefore, guard carefully the tongue.

The 6 *atmosphere* surrounding 3 also stands for education, hence this is the place to gain added knowledge. Cultivate the voice, so that you may speak or sing with ease, in any atmosphere. Happy expression through proper training is essential if 3 wishes to emerge from an ever changing, restless, emotional nature, to one of greater power and honor in the public eye. Handling a dramatic situation cleverly and with understanding may open the door to your next step.

6 also injects into the atmosphere a strong pull toward home, marriage, and children. Perhaps through such channels your larger door of opportunity may lie.

You who feel that you are going round in circles, who wish to do something different, which will improve your income and establish your social rating, would do well to observe the shorter route of arrival via 4.

THE RHYTHM OF 4

4 is the rhythm of Reason and Regularity, the 4/4 march-time which is brought into play when something definite is to be accomplished. You put your foot down with determination, you get into the swing of things. The rhythm of 4 stirs a feeling of patriotism, the idea that one is doing his duty and making a good showing thereby. This requires that one keep in line. You who may be compelled to punch a clock or move on schedule time, know that only by keeping in step can you fill your present niche and move on to the freedom of 5.

But why should the social 3, who desires to advance from his present cycle, likewise join in the march-time tread of 4?

Because every step forward is just One step more, and 3 and 1 make 4. Without the creative 1 to inject new life, no new thing can manifest.

In 4 we find the secret of advancement: *"Order is heaven's first law."* And what is this Law of Order first established in 4? That,

All growth starting in 1, moves through 3 successive stages to a definite form in 4.

In the Fourth season, winter, the grain, the result of seedtime, cultivation and harvest, contains the same inherent qualities of life as did the original seed in 1. It has the capacity to generate a new cycle of equal length and strength.

Four on every plane requires proof of statements made, hence we will let the law of Number reveal the rhythm of 4 at work in Nature and Man. (The total of each group stands below).

$$\frac{1 + 2 + 3 + 4}{\begin{matrix} 1 \quad 0 \\ 1 \end{matrix}} \qquad \frac{10 + 5 + 6 + 7}{\begin{matrix} 2 + 8 \\ 1 \quad 0 \\ 1 \end{matrix}} \qquad \frac{28 + 8 + 9 + 10}{\begin{matrix} 5 + 5 \\ 1 \quad 0 \\ 1 \end{matrix}}$$

$$\frac{55 + 11 + 12 + 13}{\begin{matrix} 9 + 1 \\ 1 \quad 0 \\ 1 \end{matrix}}$$

Growth generated in one, moving through 3 consecutive steps, reaches a definite form in 4. Here some new idea (1) must be added to improve the original pattern and carry it through to 5.

At the Fourth stage of any venture one should place business before pleasure, yet provide a time for both. Here he should keep his daily schedule, his activities, his personal appearance, and social obligations, all in perfect order; paid up to date, with no balance left over.

In 4, one must true the corners, count the cost, and bring everything down to the finest point of efficiency. But if 4 spends so much time keeping the corners clean and counting the cost, that he has no time for play, his eyes become so closely glued to his present level that he may become a drudge.

One does not grow by staying too long duty-bound, in routine over and over, any more than he does by going round and round in rhythmic cycles of 3. One must touch all the Nine paths of experience symbolized by the Nine numbers if he would become a well-rounded personality.

THE WAY OUT FOR THOSE WITH 4 IN NAME OR BIRTH

Those with 8 in Name or Birth, also take notice as 8 is twice 4.

[27]

Those with 7 also note, as 7 is 4 and 3.

Those with 22 also note, as 22 is 4 when reduced.

We are never in a situation longer than it takes to learn the lesson that it holds—hence those of you who feel bound by limitation, remember the maxim:

"Without the setting of metes and bounds
There is no coming forth."

While it may be difficult, by reason of outer pressure, to find release from your present four-square walls, your first attempt at escape should logically be, straight Up— from a quiet point in the center.

Having established Order in your affairs, arrange to keep an appointment with yourself alone, each day at a stated time. Then when quiet has eased your mind, ask counsel of your Imagination, gained in 3. Adding 3 to your present 4, you have a tower of 7 by which to mount and look beyond your present limitations. From this high point of vantage you may discern which one of your four walls is the strongest, which one of your duties has been performed so well that you may turn the routine over to another and *extend* your knowledge in a similar but larger field.

If Reason (4) and Imagination (3) do not bring the answer sought, know that in the further stillness of the intuitive 7 you may invoke the aid of your "magic rod" to reveal that talent, or duty, which offers the best way out.

Then by concentration on this One way, with a decision (1) to go forward, you so *extend your former wall* beyond its present confines, that you walk out upon it, to greet with a healthy curiosity those experiences which await you in the new freedom of 5.

COMING EVENTS CAST THEIR SHADOWS BEFORE

As coming events cast their shadows before, so does the light from the step just completed reveal the path and the reward that awaits in another like measure of time.

Thus 4, casting his shadow before, views in 8, power and wealth twice that of his present measure. Knowing that success is won more quickly when one is master of his present environment, the 4 who wishes to speed his ultimate good, sets in motion his own rhythm of *regularity*.

He admits that Time, the Fourth aspect of the physical universe, is the governing factor in his affairs. Time, reflected upon the mental plane in reason, provides a basis for his judgment.

Reason regulates the imagination and enables one to hold it for stated periods of time, focused in one direction, until the plane of intuition is touched and the picture is seen more clearly. Then, as we have found before, 3 successive stages crystalizing in 4, Reason, Imagination, and Intuition, all focused upon a given center by the Will, give birth to the flash of inspiration.

Here we have that bright light, that flash which we may be able to hold but for a moment, but having touched it once, we may again by the same process reach it in 4, and glimpse the whole Octave of 8.

Beyond 4, the rhythm of all Numbers is but some combination of 1, 2, 3 and 4.

The atmosphere of 4, despite its regular swing, is always conducive to inspiration from a new I d e a, for $1 + 2 + 3 + 4 = 10.$

$$9\ 4\ 5\ 1$$
$$1\ 9$$
$$1\ 0$$

The realization of One dream is but the beginning of another. In the measured beat of your present hour lies the reflection of tomorrow's pleasure.

Chapter V

THE RHYTHM OF LANGUAGE

THE POWER OF THE NAME

"Rhythm, which is the seed and life of life,
And of all art the root and branch and bloom"
        —is that which makes music of speech.

"Speech is air given a soul." As the Good Book says,
"Out of the fullness of the heart the mouth speaketh,"
and, as *The Song of Sano Tarot* adds, "Where no Love
sings, Service is but noise."

Speech is sound in rhythm, each tone or word having
its characteristic accent. As Sano Tarot states: "Words
are bodies of forces, which once set in motion, move on
through endless time, building or destroying, according
to the will which sent them forth.

"Moving *spiralwise*, they return in due season
and cross the lives of their creators. Set a watch at
the door of your lips, that the fruit of your words be
blessings."

Words are crystallized thought, portraying in their
accent the motive of the speaker. If you wish your words
to carry weight and be remembered, send them forth in
rhythmic measure, with the accent always in its proper
place. Is not a verse of poetry or a line oft repeated in
early youth easily remembered, and did it not make a
greater impression than the preaching or entreaty of
parent and teacher combined?

You, who in your school days, learned to sing the
multiplication table to the tune of Yankee Doodle, think
you that it developed your voice? Perhaps, but there-
after, without trying to think, all you needed to do, to

remember that 4 times 8 was 32, was to recall the tune, and as you fell in line with its rhythm, the answer fell into your mind, without any effort whatever.

Thus may you invoke the principle of rhythm—even the advertisers are doing it now—if you wish your counsel or teaching to be happily remembered.

Rhythm is based on accent, accent upon the relation of one note to another in the same measure. Measure can only be determined by Number. Therefore, to find the rhythm of any word, we must know the number of letters it contains, and where to place the accent.

In all alphabets, the letters stand in a certain order. In English, German, and some other languages they are numbered from 1 to 26, in Hebrew from 1 to 22, in Greek from 1 to 24. The position thus established determines the number value of the letter, in its relation to the others.

In the early languages, such as Hebrew, Greek, and Chaldee, before numerals came into use, letters and numbers were interchangeable. The meaning of a word or name was derived from the number-letters which formed it. Words of a similar number value bore a relation to each other, as synonym or antonym.

THE MEANING OF THE NUMBERS

The basic meaning of the numbers, reflected in language everywhere, represents man's concept of the evolution of the cosmos. The first three reflect the creative Trinity, the seven following, the "Seven Spirits around the throne," the Seven planets, reflected in nature by the Seven colors of the rainbow, Seven notes of the musical scale, Seven days of the week, and Seven important centers of the body.

In Hebrew much importance was laid to the fact that Yod-He-Vau-He, the name of Jehovah, composed of the 10th, 5th, 6th and 5th letters of the alphabet, totaled 26 or 8. Using a similar law of correspondence, numbering the English alphabet, reducing all above 9 by adding their digits (z the 26th letter is $2 + 6 = 8$), we have:

A B C D E F G H I   J K L M N O P Q R
1 2 3 4 5 6 7 8 9   1 2 3 4 5 6 7 8 9
S T U V W X Y Z
1 2 3 4 5 6 7 8

Thus we find that G o d totals 8, and in German,
$$7 6 4 = 1 + 7 = 8$$

G o t t is also 8.
$$7 6 2 2 = 17 = 8$$

As a C r e a t o r and B u i l d e r did God
3 9 5 1 2 6 9   2 3 9 3 4 5 9
$3 5 = 8$ $3 5 = 8$
bring his original P l a n, reflected in the Seven
$$7 3 1 5 = 16 = 7$$
aspects of N a t u r e,   into
$$5 1 2 3 9 5 = 25 = 7$$
a c t i o n,   in measured law and order.
$$1 3 2 9 6 5 = 26 = 8.$$

Those familiar with the tenets of Masonry will be
familiar with the meaning of the numbers, as shown there,
where the Pythagorean teaching aims to show that
*through an understanding of number, one finds the unity
underlying all things.*

The general interpretation of numbers as symbols of
universal principles are shown below. Other applica-
tions are but some variation of their fundamental
character.

1—Spirit—Masculine—Will, acting through Decision.
2—Soul—Feminine—Wisdom, co-ordinating through
   Memory.
3—Mind—Imagination — Understanding — Reproduc-
   tive Intelligence.
4—Body—Form—Plan — Limitation — Substance —
   Foundation.
5—Man, reaching out through his Five senses for Experience; Investigation developing Intuition.
6—Discrimination—Beauty—Creation—The Home.
7—Victory—Authority—Finish — Perfection — Recognition—Withdrawal.

[32]

8—Splendor—Power through Justice and establishment of Balance between Intellect and Emotion.
9—Love—Service—Humanity—The World.
10—Kingdom of Attainment—Masculine and Feminine in perfect Balance.

THE MASTER NUMBERS: 11, 22, 33

While we have only nine digits, there are three higher numbers indicative of mastery on three planes: 11, 22 and 33, comparable to three cycles of growth and development in every human being.

From 1 to 10, physical growth is dominant.

From 11 to 22 the mental gains in strength. At 21, the boy is given the right to vote; at 22 he leaves college.

From 22 to the early thirties a higher consciousness develops in his contact with the world.

Thus does 11 mark that dynamic energy found in the virile youth, who just entering upon the mental plane of action, views all things in a new light. 11 has that power of quick decision which enables him to take in a situation at a glance, anticipate the next move, and lead the way. 11 stands as a Light to inaugurate a "new beginning."

22 represents the development of reason and diplomacy. There are 22 white keys in three octaves on the piano. It gives a wide range of activity. In correlating the physical with the mental 22 strives to find a reason for all things, and make even the inspirational, spiritual concepts, practical.

33 is the spiritual consciousness developed through experience and a desire for a higher plane of Service. This we will leave for the 33rd degree Mason to interpret.

THE POWER OF THE NAME

The Power of the Name has always been held of great importance in every religion. The outstanding characters in both the Old and New Testaments had a change of name when there was a change of consciousness, as did Saul, when upon his conversion his name was changed to Paul.

In Mark 3:14-17, we read that when the Master chose his twelve disciples and ordained them, "to preach, and to have power to heal sicknesses and to cast out devils, . . . Simon, he surnamed Peter; and James, the son of Zebedee, and John his brother, he surnamed Boanerges, which is, The sons of thunder."

Thus did he exemplify the truth of the principle that *your name identifies you*, revealing to the outside world the character of your inner consciousness. In giving his three close disciples, the highest initiates of the Twelve, an entirely new last name, he cut them loose from their old associations and gave them a new vibration with which to attract and express a higher state of consciousness.

ANCIENT FREEMASONRY—GEMATRIA

In *Ancient Freemasonry*, by Frank Higgins, we find that Freemasonry is considered by some to be the parent of all religions, and that, "The key to the entire secret system (concealed from the masses by the priesthood, because it was too high for them to grasp), is found in the ancient method of using identical characters for letters and numbers, a system called Gematria."

Mr. Higgins continues: "One of the hardest things to explain to the average mind, well stored with the rudiments of the arts and sciences, as taught in the schools, is that there *are phases* of all the popular sciences, which are just as real as anything they have ever learned but which have not been included in the domain of popular education for many hundreds of years . . . as they consist of those mathematical and geometrical common factors to all sciences from which our forefathers deduced their theory, nay certainty, of a unique divine law pervading the entire universe, from the systems of suns and stars, to the molecular structure of an almost invisible world, revealed by the microscope.

"That *the Science of Numbers is the One Thing* which can be truly said to pervade time, space, quantity or volume, and proportion."

Chapter VI

OTHER LANGUAGES

The interpretation of a name or word in different languages by its number value, shows the characteristic attitude with which different nationalities regard the same thing.

Using as a brief example the words shown below, one may discern the difference of opinion existing between Germany and The States, as to woman's place in the home.

	Wife		*Home*	
Total Vowels	5	4	5	11
	Wife	Frau	Heim	Home
Total Consonants	11	6	3	3
Total Word	7	10	8	5

Mother		*Children*		*Father*	
11	8	5	5	6	6
Mother	Mutter	Children	Kinder	Vater	Father
5	8	5	2	6	7
7	7	10	7	3	4

"Mother" in both languages totals 7, representing the completion and perfection of the home, and the refining, intuitive, spiritual influence which she lends to the environment.

Both "wife" and "mother" in English have the 11-5-7 inspirational, intuitive trinity. But note that the 5 and 11 are reversed. The American man, as a rule, looks to his mother for inspiration (11) or sympathy, but he is more eager for his wife to make a good showing in the limelight (11 consonant) as this naturally reflects greater credit upon himself.

The American wife has a greater urge for freedom (5 vowel), and enjoys more recognition (7 total) than does the German wife, whose duties (4) demand her concentrated attention. Due to her larger family (6 consonant), she may have so many problems (10) at home that she does not have a chance to exercise the spirit of adventure (11-5-7) found in the majority of young matrons in America.

The German mother is thrifty and a good "general" (8)—American mothers are too, but generally speaking the German *heim* (8) is run upon a more definite working schedule than the home in America, where the 5 (total), indicative of freedom, makes for a more variable, changeable atmosphere.

"Father" totals 4. His duty is to lay a foundation (4) of financial support for the family, and he is generally kept quite busy (4) in that capacity. "Vater," with a total of 3, attracts comfort, good food, and attention to his physical needs. His voice (6 appearing twice) is heard more than that of the American father, who may often be absent (7 consonant) by reason of necessary concentration upon his work (4).

As for the children, there is no comparison between the freedom (5) of thought and action among the younger generation in America and those on the continent. There, obedience (2 consonant) is required. The 7 of "Kinder" reflects the concept that "children should be seen, not heard." Theirs is a more inhibited (7) environment than that of the children of the U. S. A. whose expression of independence is proverbial.

YOUR NATIONALITY

Whatever may be your nationality, you have inherited traits of consciousness in keeping with your birthplace. No matter how long since you changed your name, or moved to a foreign clime, your natural traits of character are revealed in the name as given at birth.

In analyzing an Italian we number the letters of the Italian alphabet (reducing those above 9 by adding their digits) and put the corresponding number under each letter of the name. In analyzing a Greek we would use their 24-letter alphabet in like manner.

Thus do we find that rhythm of sound energy which first made its impress upon the sensitive nature of the child, bringing its later reflex in instinctive reaction to people or things.

Chapter VII

YOU AND YOUR FRIENDS

Would you believe it?
—It matters not,
We'll endeavor to explain—
That in the letters of your Name
We find your Destiny and Aim,
But that a greater secret still
Lies in the Birthdate, if you will,
Which points the Way to fame.

In the song of life, you have been given a special part, happiness is an art.

In your Full Birth Name, the Words of your song are written, while in your Birthdate lies the Key and the rhythmic swing of your harmony.

Some people move in one key, while others move in another—this is termed Individuality.

All keys are good, but not good for all people. We do not feel at home with those whose tone is sharp or flat in comparison with our own. Should we both express our views at once, both would be thrown off pitch.

One must first determine his Octave and Key before he can hope to enjoy harmony with other personalities or their plans.

YOU—THE OCTAVE OF YOUR NAME

Your *Full Birth Name*, composed of letters from the alphabet of your native tongue, reveals your natural range. your dominant notes, and the keys which may be missing. For those who wish to delve further into the Why of things, you will find Eight aspects worth considering, based on the full birth name:

Your Destiny and type of mind *in its total.*
Your Soul quality, talents, and subconscious desires in its total *vowels.*
Your Instinctive Reaction to people or things in the *first vowel.*
Your Personality—appearance to the outside world—in the total *consonants.*
Your Heredity in the total of *last name.*
Your Individuality in total of *first* and *middle names.*
Your Habit of Thinking, reflected in your peculiarities, in the *number of letters* in the name.
Your Missing Notes in the *numbers lacking* in your name.

People really take you at your Number rather than your face value.

Why? Because the rhythm of your name, repeated again and again, sets up certain mental and physical reflexes which eventually become habit, registering upon the outside world as Personality and Character.

Your *present mental attitude* is seen in the signature most frequently used. such rhythm attracting the friends and experiences of your present environment.

Your *nickname* represents You to those who address you thus. Note its total Number if you wish to know your special standing.

As every number has its opposite aspects, day and night being but One Day on the calendar, someone whose name is identical with your own may be opposite in both disposition and material success, living on the dark side of his vibration while you are in the light.

Your Name is your best advertising medium for letting the world hear and know of your good qualities. You are to the world what your name portrays, but inwardly you may be an entirely different person;—

This *hidden* quality, established on your date of birth by the inrushing wave of air which set your physical machinery in motion, reveals that Inner Urge which is ever seeking outward expression. In its particular rhythm and accent lies the secret of Your Buried Treasure, and the avenues by which it can best be uncovered. These are observed more fully in a later chapter.

YOUR FRIENDS—1, 2, 3, 4, 5, 6, 7, 8, 9, 10, 11, 22

Who are your Friends—everywhere?

How can you make new ones?

And understand those you have?

You are the harpist in your world, playing upon an instrument of many strings, bringing back a vibrant response, in keeping with your skillful touch.

But until you know the scale, no great varieties of harmonies may be played. There are Seven notes in the musical scale and Five black keys, making Twelve tones in One octave. As there are Seven colors in the rainbow, with Five additional, coming from a blend of the varied shades; as there are Seven centers of the body and Five of kindred importance; as there are Seven months from seedtime to harvest and Five additional, making Twelve to complete the full cycle of the year, so are there Seven kinds of people into which the majority of humanity fall—1-2-3-4-5-6-7, the other Five representing the leadership class, less in number, but with greater individual strength and power—8-9-10-11-22.

Being born in one class does not require that you remain there—The broader your experience, the more will you be able to find a point of harmony with each one of the Twelve.

Knowing the key to which another responds and the rhythm he enjoys, you have at your command a boomerang. Be gentle in your play.

If you wish a true reward, *be natural!* Only thus will you be able to touch the true self of the other. Seek not to merely please, pacify, improve, or advise. Unless your own harp of Twelve strings be in tune, you may expect a discordant note somewhere.

It will be difficult for another to recognize in you his true soul mate if you be out of rhythm with the tempo in which you both should move. A soul mate may be a happy find, yet lacking such desired estate, compatibility in the home or professional world is worth striving for.

Knowing your own dominant notes, you have the power to include all others within your range. When

[40]

this point has been reached, the quality of music emitted by your soul will be that melodious harmony which springs from one who plays with skill, ease, and understanding, not only upon Twelve strings, but upon the whole gamut of human emotion.

Having mastered the scale, one step at a time, you may go up and down with ease—and be at home, in any clime, with every kind of human nature, anywhere.

Chapter VIII

ONE IN ALL

THREE STEPS TO YOUR HEART'S DESIRE

One, as a part of every Number, has some characteristics common to all. This gives you, with the One vibration in Name or Birth, a connecting link with every type of mind. You should find in everyone some note of interest or kindred response, and in turn they should receive a stimulus to new endeavor through you.

Living on your constructive side, guided by your intuition, moving straight toward your goal, unaffected by praise or blame from friend or foe, you should find in every successful soul you meet some quality which, if added to your own, will take you One step further. Seek it out!

In one who is floundering you may see reflected some quality of your own nature which has not yet been wisely directed. Set it straight!

In every failure you may observe a good quality, gone too far in the wrong direction—or totally neglected.

With the strong creative power at your command, you may build your own Utopia (or its opposite), according to the strength of your decision and well-directed effort.

What would You, or your friends among the other Numbers, *love to do, have,* or *be?*

"Where your treasure is, there will your heart be also."

Your heart generates life. With no heart in your work, it becomes as dead timber. With love in your heart no task is too difficult, no way too long. Love is the motive power which moves you in the swiftest period of time from where you are to where you wish to be.

The heaven of your heart's desire may not be reached

in a single bound, but for you, as well as for all the other numbers, it comes when you have touched all steps from 1 to 9 and reach, in 10, the Kingdom of Attainment. One being the farthest removed from Nine, you have the longest journey before you. But here's a secret! Because of your excellent balance of both masculine and feminine traits, your receptivity to new ideas and the initiative to carry them through, you can go farther alone than any of the other Numbers.

Though alone, you will not be lonesome. Life will be a new adventure when, setting in motion the rhythm of your heart's desire, instead of moving slowly from 1 to 9, you gain your objective in Three swift bounds.

How?

1st: LOVE YOURSELF! Love is the all-inclusive 9. *You* are 1, and the only One in this world for whom you are entirely responsible. Setting in rhythm the vibration of Love around yourself, the blend of 1 and 9 makes 10— and you have already touched the keynote of your Kingdom of Attainment. You have established its center of gravity, right where you are.

To love yourself means to cease self-condemnation. Think well enough of your talents and your higher intuition to carry out the ideas that are coming through *immediately*—before someone else with a like wave length sets a kindred idea into operation and reaps the reward which might have been yours.

Loving yourself, all things take on a different hue. You have more tolerance with those who have a less advanced point of view—you don't expect them to agree with you. You know that each one has his own niche to fill.

Standing firmly on your own center, shining brightly where you are, as a pivot in the center of your universe, you may turn your light (attention) in any direction, and its good-will rays, striking the path of another, will cast a warming beam and attract *your own* in abundant measure.

2nd: LOVE WHAT YOU ARE NOW DOING. Why? Because Love relaxes. If you *love to do* it, there is no resentment,

[43]

no tension, you are through in less time, and all things move more smoothly. Without an atmosphere of Love in which to flow, your intuition is impeded—for the best ideas, it must have a free and open channel. These in turn point the way to a new and higher level.

3rd: LOVE EACH ONE YOU MEET until you understand him, and then it will be much easier to love him more.

Why? Because however difficult or impossible he may be, he reflects one of the basic types of human nature. He is somewhere on the ladder of achievement from 1 to 22. If you have mastered his round he cannot trouble or annoy you—you will know how to handle him. But if you have the lesson of his vibration yet to learn, love him for the opportunity he affords for your next advancement in Understanding. Hereafter all other like characters will be as flecks on the surface compared to him.

With a knowledge of all types, based on experience, your divining rod of Intuition becomes ever more swift in uncovering for you the hidden wealth in any association and pointing the way to the next best step.

When you can meet every type of human nature in the spirit of Love, knowing him for what he really is, and his particular place on the ladder, you no longer expect the impossible from those who are children in Understanding. You love them as you would your own spoiled child, and with no resentment or ill-will to hold you back, you go swiftly forward to the realization of your heart's desire, which is yours the moment you have mastered the intervening rounds.

Chapter IX

YOUR HIDDEN TREASURE

Did you know that within you lies treasure far greater than you have yet uncovered? That you are a highly sensitized electrical instrument more intricate than anything yet devised? That your mind is the motor which makes things go? That your name shows your particular type of instrument and purpose here, while your birth date reveals the energy rate at your command?

As the smooth functioning of any electrical device, and its efficiency, depend upon the right contact and outlet for its current of power, so do your health, success and happiness depend upon the proper outlet for your particular type of energy. The ease with which your task is accomplished and your freshness for the coming day rest upon your perfect understanding of the technique required and happy adjustment to your environment.

All machinery is said to work better when given a rest one day in seven, but for the higher type of instrument known as Man, in the New Day now dawning, four days of work, one day for investigation in new fields, or for going places; one day given to home or education, and one day of rest, will comprise that week which, in rhythm with the purpose of nature, will make for a more efficient growth within and a greater universal love without.

Granting that such a Utopia is in view, how may we employ our time to bring the greatest return? Even now, many of us work twice as hard as is needed. One who continually rows up stream or in a cross current puts forth twice the effort of one who moves with the tide. There is an economic current in the world of affairs, 'tis

[45]

true, but there is also an individual stream of energy in which your activities should flow if you wish things to run smoothly and successfully.

This current, based on the wave of energy in motion at the time you made your start—your first appearance on this planet, is found in your date of birth. On that day the calendar registered a certain month, day and year, which reduced to a single number, shows the energy rate of that day. This current, to which your body is attuned, continues to flow through you until the end. Upon its efficient handling depends your happiness and success, from the cradle to the grave. At no time should it be allowed to drop below par, its original energy rate.

Following your birth, the next important event was the Name you attracted. In this we find the key to your early environment, your heredity and family tree. Upon the blend of what you *can do*, revealed by your name, with what your Inner Self *desires*, shown in date of birth, rests the beauty of your life pattern. Both must be given consideration.

MULTIPLY YOUR GOOD BY TWO

Until you can do two things well, one that comes naturally, and one acquired (in keeping with your Birthpath urge), you will never be that well balanced individual who stands supreme in his world, above all tides of economic depression.

With only one avenue open, you must of necessity rise and fall with the energy waves about you, but with two, you can balance yourself, as it were, on the two opposite poles, and let the tide roll between, under, or over, and still hold your ground.

Until you can see two sides of a subject you are not prepared to judge the point of balance in the middle. Every high school and college should equip the graduate to earn his living by at least two different routes. With two occupations (two of anything blended produce a third) there is always a third in the offing. This, crystallized and blended with the first, produces a fourth, and so on, *ad infinitum*. But until you have at least Two,

[46]

you have no means of multiplying your good; you are subject to the wind and wave of prosperity or adversity.

When you become as a highly tempered piece of steel, able to bend but not break, your talent becomes more adaptable to the varied needs of the present era, whose trend is shown in a recent book on *Power Sales* (Taylor) : "It becomes more apparent every day that the major problems facing the power salesman are not strictly *electrical*, but rather *mechanical* and *economic*. . . . The largest elements in providing industrial power are mechanical. The largest problems in replacing private generation with purchased power are economic." The electrically trained engineer must deal with two other fields to handle his own successfully.

3

22

50

22

3

IN WHICH CLASS ARE YOU?

"After endless research among many classes and groups it has been found that of every 100 persons, taken as you will, young or old, educated or illiterate, mechanics or bankers, college students or sailors, 50 will be *just average folks*, 22 below the average and 3 below that. Moving to the right, 22 will be above the average, and 3 above that—exceptional, remarkable prodigies. This holds not only of intelligence, but of moral character, health and strength, geniality, etc."

The above statistics were taken from a periodical unfamiliar with the hidden meaning of 22 as a master number. The 22 keys in three octaves on the piano represent completion or perfection in three cycles or fields of effort. The singer who has a range beyond three octaves is considered most exceptional, a genius indeed.

If you wish to join the group which stands above the average, perfect yourself in Three lines. 7 stands for perfection in one line. $3 \times 7 = 21$. 22 marks the turn into a new cycle, for those few who can go still higher.

[47]

For the average on the higher levels it stands as the high point of achievement, broad contacts, and broad view.

Every Number offers a special field for success. The 11 and 22 give added power in the direction of the other numbers shown.

Chapter X

BLEND YOUR TALENTS WITH YOUR BIRTHPATH URGE

Your Name reveals your talents and your powers of attraction in the outer world. It shows your level of consciousness or understanding, which enables you to make friends among a certain class. But admitting that you have a Name vibration of 6, if your Birthpath be 7, an entirely different rhythm—two different rates of energy operating at the same time, one active, the other more passive, exclusive and retiring, what would you do about it?

That is the question,—to so understand the opposing forces in your own nature that you can blend them into a harmonious whole and give to each their share of opportunity.

The reason most of us do not *arrive* sooner, is that we change our minds too often as to what our goal should really be. We are like the boy who started to build a snowman in the likeness of George Washington. Before Washington was completed he decided to mould Lincoln. Before Abraham's whiskers were finished he resolved to make a Roosevelt, but before Roosevelt was finished the *Sun* came out, melted his snowman, and he had nothing to show for his effort.

Thus many a one works continuously without any great reward, because the several sides of his nature are all clamoring for expression at the same time. When one gives to each particular urge its proper time and attention, peace and harmony begin to reign. The dreams which before were always "just around the corner" come within reach.

Do not try to follow a line of endeavor for which you

have no natural qualifications, nor allow others to persuade you in such direction. The moment an airplane tries to carry a load beyond its capacity, not only does it have difficulty in "taking off," but if it really does get started, nine times out of ten there is a crash.

The same is true of any individual who tries to go beyond his strength or swim in a current for which his nature is not adapted. There is said to be a species of deep sea fish which will burst if they venture into too shallow water, where the pressure is lighter. There is no reason why any of us should have such an inglorious end. Find your own pressure and the current in which you should move. Pressure from without cannot harm you if properly gauged to that within. When the inner force is balanced, the outer pressure only strengthens the individuality.

Your *Inner* force is found in your *Date of Birth*, the MONTH governing *Physical* growth for first 12 years. Your *DAY* rules *Mental* development from 13 to 25, as one goes through High School and college. The *YEAR* brings *Emotional* development from 25 to 36, when one marries or starts a career. At 37, your *TOTAL BIRTH-DATE* reflects that *INNER URGE* found in one's *LIFE WORK*.

Your *Outer* pressure is seen in your *Name*. When this is in rhythm with, and as high as Birthdate or higher, it affords a normal outlet for the energy coming through. You have a center of balance and poise that makes for peace within and success without. In harmony with yourself, moving in the direction of your deep desire, you can hope and expect to find a joyous outlet for your talents.

Your normal rate of vibration, the energy for which you must find a constructive outlet, is found in your date of birth, in the addition of month, day and year.

Your Name is your contact point with the outside world and affords the outlet for the urge within. If smaller than your Birthpath, the repression of normal energy may bring irritation in health or affairs. If too high for your Birthpath, you may not have sufficient energy to carry out your ambition or grasp opportunities offered.

Your NAME, like the Treble clef in music, is your MELODY, each letter a note, and Number in the alphabet.

```
1 2 3 4 5 6 7 8 9    j k l m n o p q r    s t u v w x y z
a b c d e f g h i    1 2 3 4 5 6 7 8 9    1 2 3 4 5 6 7 8
```

DWIGHT   DAVID   EISENHOWER — 34th President
```
459782   41494   5915586559
 ‾‾35‾‾            ‾‾58‾‾ ‾‾−13‾‾
   8   +   *22       +       4      = (34) — DESTINY
       8 + 4 = 12 = 3 + 22 =      (3—22)
```
With a *34* Destiny, is it by chance that we find here the 34th President of the U N I T E D   S T A T E S , whose
```
                    359254  121251
                    ‾‾28‾‾ =10 ‾‾+  12‾‾ = (22)
```
genial smile has enabled him to make *friends* (3) with
```
   3        22
```
all classes everywhere. His love for G o l f is seen in *22 of* both Name and Birth.   7 6 3 6 = 2 2

The BIRTHDATE (Bass clef), marks the basic rhythm of one's career at different periods in the life. One with *22* in Name or birth, like the 22 White keys in 3 octaves on piano, has a wider range of action than the average and more ability to mould others to his view.

Born in Libra October 14 1890
```
        7 + 10 + 5    18              SPIRIT
        ‾‾‾22‾‾ +    9 = (22–9) Inner Urge
```
The unusual leadership in Three Octaves is shown:

1. As G E N E R A L , in rhythm with D W I G H T
```
   7 5 5 5 9 1 3
   ‾‾35‾‾ =   8                          3 5 = 8
```
and Libra-October.
```
   7 + 1
   ‾‾8‾‾
```

2. As President of C O L U M B I A University in rhythm
```
                    3 6 3 3 4 2 9 1 with EISENHOWER,
                    ‾‾31‾‾ =   4              4
```
3. As President of UNITED STATES (22), in rhythm with Full Name. His leadership in WORLD (9) affairs fulfills both his Destiny and 22-9 Urge of his Life Pattern.

* Master numbers 22 and 11 indicate leadership in direction of others. Totals shown. Add remaining numbers.

[51]

THOMAS ALVA EDISON
2 8 6 4 1 1   1 3 4 1   5 4 9 1 6 5
            9   30

                      12
  22   +   3   = (22–3) — DESTINY
                               7

A M a s t e r in realm of e l e c t r i c i t y , whose
411259   5 3 5 3 2 9 9 3 9 2 7
  22   57 = 12
                                 3
C o u r a g e
3 6 3 9 1 7 5
  34
   7   and Tenacity (7) brought to perfection his
many creative efforts. Working in harmony with his natural talent, (3 last name), he gained recognition as a master workman in his field.
    The 22 of Thomas gave him the b r o a d vision and
                              2 9 6 1 4 = 2 2

natural equipment to handle his high powered birthdate,
really a double 22.
    Born in Aquarius February 11, 1847
                 2   20
        *11 + 11‾22 =(11–11–22) — URGE
               6   8
    The Four master numbers in Birthdate show
unusual power. As C r e a t o r of the incandescent
           3 9 5 1 2 6 9
                3 5 = 8
L i g h t and his many other epoch making inven-
3 9 7 8 2
  29 = 11
tions he literally revolutionized the world and gave
S p e e d to its progress.
1 7 5 5 4 = 2 2
    In the 2 and 20 of Month and Year he made his great
contribution to M u s i c . In "His Master's Voice,"—
             43193 =20
through the phonograph and its myriad subsequent devel-

* For number of Your Natal Sign, see page 56.

[52]

opments. the 6 undertone of main birthpath "let his voice be heard,"—the mission of 6 in any birthdate.

Six also stands for the Home, the Community, and higher Educational Standards. *Eleven* represents Light, Illumination, and New Beginnings. Through the incandescent globe, Mr. Edison brought new light to both home and community. In stimulating the establishment of night schools, it made education available to the masses. In service and pleasure, it has done more to lighten the burdens and add to the beauty of life than almost any other one invention—a fitting achievement for the triple power of mastery in Mr. Edison's name and birth—22, 11-22.

PLAY ON YOUR OWN KEY!

Master your own scale of possibilities. If you have an urge to be an artist, it will be a waste of Father's money to send you to law school. If you prefer to be a farmer, why study medicine? Give attention to your particular rhythm. Do not attempt to tune in with those individuals or places that are not on your wavelength, if you wish to attract *your own* in congenial activity and friends.

The tragedies in life are the introverts, the high power reversed, gone in the wrong direction, or totally neglected. No matter what the age, it is not too late to turn around and set your sail to catch the gale which will send you in the right direction. You have come to know the thrill of finding Hidden Treasure. May the following pages be a glass-bottomed boat for you.

Chapter XI

VOCATIONS—AVOCATIONS—FAMOUS PEOPLE

To awaken interest in the development of an Avocation, a "subordinate occupation," or personal hobby, which may later become a profitable avenue of expression for you, we are giving in the Vocations which follow, the diversified aspects of each Number. You never can tell what door will open when once you are thoroughly familiar with two or more lines.

Fritz Kreisler, famous violinist, previously was an army officer and electrician. Caesar Cui, a Russian composer, was an instructor in a military school. The rhythmic beat of the march registered later in the higher and more sensitive octave of perfected musical expression.

Whatever your Name or Birth, you have a varied choice. However, it may be well to observe a few of the successful people whose rhythm is akin to your own. We do not ask you to believe or accept the idea presented, but we do suggest, as a matter of curiosity, that you spend an evening or two with *Who's Who* and note how the activities of the famous folk are in harmony with their dominant rhythm.

Many times the surname appears to have exerted a stronger influence than the Destiny (full birth name) or Birthpath. In the last name at birth we find those deep seated hereditary traits and tendencies which, if they be in rhythm with the Birthpath, should make one a genius, but if of an entirely different nature may be the cause of many an inner conflict.

In a recent *Who's Who* we observed the name Curtis

29 times. "Curtis" adds to 9, with a 3 vowel and 6 consonant. 3-6-9 is the trinity of numbers which stands for fluency of expression in literary, artistic, or humitarian lines. 3 is the literary number; 6 gives a strong urge for education, expression, and the establishment of higher standards. We find that the majority of publishers predominate in the 6 vibration. 9 is the large, broad, world view, not forgetting the human emotions. The Curtis Publishing Company, with its three magazines, *The Saturday Evening Post*, *The Ladies Home Journal* and *The Country Gentleman*, carries in its name, in *Curtis* and *Publishing*, the 3-6-9 trinity twice, while in its more abbreviated usage, "Curtis Publishing Co." it appears four times. Its three fold message has truly penetrated to all four corners of the globe. 3-6-9 also is able to bring back a pleasing reaction from the public, and in the continued popularity of its publications, this too holds true.

Of the 29 noted people listed under *Curtis*, there were 11 writers, 9 educators, 8 lawyers and 1 artist. Nearly all writers were equally famous as educators, and vice versa. Several were M.D.'s and institutional heads. Others combined writing with art and nearly all had enjoyed world travel—touching success, not only in one, but in the three fields represented by the 3-6-9 of the name carried.

ODD OR EVEN

Generally speaking, if in your Destiny and Birthpath the Odd Numbers predominate (1-3-5-7-9-11), you belong in creative, artistic, selling or promotional effort. If Even Numbers (2-4-6-8-22) prevail, you are here to master detail and then grow from that into the more authoritative and executive positions of business manager, engineer, builder in any field who goes by rule and measure.

The Odd Numbers should work independently so far as possible and be the means of introducing, selling or perfecting new ideas for the Even Numbers to manufacture.

YOUR NATAL SIGN

Did you know that before 1752, when our present calendar was adopted, *New Years* fell on March 25th? George Washington's birthday, celebrated February 22, 1732, in the family Bible was written February 11, 1731.

January as *Month "1"* is very young in time, but the SIGNS have stood in their respective order for millions of years and have made a much deeper groove in the ethers. Without the number of the Sign,—Aries as 1, Taurus 2, Gemini 3, prefixed to Birthdate, we feel no true Vocational delineation can be made. Each SIGN has its own TONE and COLOR, reflecting the native's basic *TEMPERAMENT.*

	Natal SIGN	*TONE*	*COLOR*
1—ARIES	Mar. 22-Apr. 20	C	*RED*—Vitality, daring pioneer, energy, impulsive, ardent.
2—TAURUS	Apr. 21-May 21	C♯ D♭	*Red-Orange* — Active mentality, born analyst, enduring, pride.
3—GEMINI	May 22-June 21	D	*ORANGE* — Mental stimulant, aid to weak lungs. Changeable, talented, devoted to family.
4—CANCER	June 22-July 22	D♯ E♭	*Yellow-Orange* — Spiritual aspirations, yet practical. Tenacious, often a duty complex.
5—LEO	July 23-Aug. 23	E	*YELLOW* — Proud, good intellect. Can meet public. Enjoys other sex and own high place in Sun.

	Natal SIGN	TONE	COLOR
6—VIRGO	Aug. 24-Sept. 23	F	*Yellow-Green* — Thrives on responsibility. Loves home, music, drama. Industrious, helpful.
7—LIBRA	Sept. 24-Oct. 23	F♯ Gb	*GREEN* — Adaptable, intuitive, understanding, persistent.
8—SCORPIO	Oct. 24-Nov. 21	G	*Blue-Green* — Strong feeling, strong mind. Often conflict between head and heart. Dauntless.
9—SAGITTARIUS	Nov. 22-Dec. 21	G♯ Ab	*BLUE* — Devotion to noble ideal. Travel good for health and spirit.
10—CAPRICORN	Dec. 22-Jan. 20	A	*Blue-Violet* — Deep feeling on high things, yet practical, cautious.
11—AQUARIUS	Jan. 21-Feb. 19	A♯ Bb	*VIOLET* — Artistic, inventive, Truth-seeker, ahead of time.
12—PISCES	Feb. 20-Mar. 21	B	*Red-Violet*—Sacrificial to cause or family. Need encouragement.

Vocation—Activity in Creative lines, where Foresight, Intuition and Initiative enable one to make a quick decision.

Professions—Creative artist in music, opera, on radio, or stage. Writer, illustrator, designer, architect. Originator advertising ideas or new methods of service. Neurologist, psychiatrist, surgeon, diagnostician, character analyst, lawyer, politician, one who keeps in touch with the "pulse" of individual or community. Aviator, geographer, guide, weather-man, "prophet" in any field, able to locate oil or water, or whose intuitive knowledge of future trends is of value now.

Business—Inventor, manufacturer, contractor, promoter, originator of new methods or system, the first to put a new product on market. Credit man, inspector, telephone operator, personnel worker, puzzle-maker. Director advertising, employment, or entertainment service—the Idea-man (or woman) who stimulates the "conservatives" and sets a new pace.

Avocation—Artist, actor, designing own clothes, new methods of entertainment; finding new places of interest. Write something for the newspaper expressing your views. Take an interest in politics; look up the political leader in your community and learn the trend of the political weather—it might possibly blow something your way. Invent new ways of being different. Analyze your friends by their Name and Number.

10—the FIRST in his field.

10 Names—ALEXANDER GRAHAM BELL

$$3 \;+\; 3 \;+\; 4 = (10).$$

Inventor of *Telephone* (10).

WINSTON CHURCHILL (6 + 4 = 10).

A-1 in *Writing* (10) and *Politics* (4).

10 Birth—*Albert Schweitzer* Capr. Jan. 14 1875*

Noted pioneer (10) 10 1 5 3

Doctor (3) in 11 + 8

Africa (11). = (11–8)

10

* Add Year,—general field of activity. 1875=21=(3).

NUMBER 2—THE ANALYST

Vocation—Activity calling for tact, co-operation and system in blending ideas, materials or people. *Two* should not try to work alone. His success lies in the ability to analyze and associate harmoniously with others.

Professions—Statesman, diplomat, politician. Movie actor, musician, composer, theatrical producer, director or member of chorus, group or orchestra. Poet, sculptor, art collector, director of Museum, landscape artist, architect. Novelist, columnist, correspondent, publisher, librarian, biographer, genealogist, lexicographer. Physicist, bacteriologist, assayer, gold mining engineer. Character analyst, club organizer, director of tours.

Business—Statistician, collector, merchant, importer or exporter. Insurance adjuster, renting or booking agent, arbitrator. Secretary, stenographer, clerk, filing or detail expert. In police, detective, traffic, mail, or civil service. Manager of tours, matrimonial bureau, chain of movie houses, beauty parlors, shoe, hosiery or stationery stores. Active in group, or co-operative movements. Gold miner.

Avocation—Collecting anything that suits your fancy —stamps, time pieces, gold coins, rare books, first editions, programs, miniatures. Study human nature and be an analyst. Starting socially, your avocation may later become a vocation. Develop your musical talent; attend musicales, play that you are a critic, write up your own review, then compare it with the professional account next day.

20—MUSIC—RULE—SYSTEM

20 *Names*—LUDWIG VAN BEETHOVEN
$$4 + 10 + 6 = (20).$$ Composer.
CAESAR. *Caesar Petrillo*, Musician's Union.

20 *Birth*—Composers *Handel* and *Bach* born in 1685=**20,**

Sibelius, Finnish composer, in 1865=**20,**
Mozart in Aquarius Jan. 27, 1756, an **11–20,**
R. Babson, Cancer July 6, 1875*
Statistican, and $4 + 7 + 6 + 3 = (20)$.
Business Analyst.

* Add Year.

Vocation—Activity which provides opportunity for expression of one's talents creatively, where ability to make friends and a sense of humor are indispensable.

Professions—Writer, society editor, humorist, entertainer, movie actor, magician, dancer, member of chorus, professional bridge player. Artist, illustrator, designer, cartoonist, photographer, landscape gardener. Doctor (women or children's specialist), nurse, chemist, pharmacist, cosmetician, dietitian, food expert, horticulturist. Lawyer, linguist, lecturer, evangelist, promoter, advertising or newspaper man. Director kindergarten, playground or welfare activities; social secretary.

Business—Correspondent, social sponsor, club host (or hostess). Manager tea room, restaurant, delicatessen, grocery, health food store. Druggist, perfumer, dealer in gifts, toys, novelties, candy, food or electrical supplies. Electrician, worker in arts and crafts, weaver. Dressmaker, beauty expert. Salesman (or woman) of millinery, lingerie, dresses, children's wear, sporting goods, art, or amusement service, news publications. A genial aid in health, hospital or welfare activities.

Avocation—Entertainer, designer—place cards, lamp shades, novelties, cartoons, posters, toys, added touches of color for children's wear; writer of bed-time stories. Try your hand at making candy, decorating furniture, weaving. Send in the recipe for your best dish to a column and add to your fun and pin money. Study languages. Visit hospital and lend cheer to patients. Add to your fund of after-dinner stories, exercise your bump of humor. Cultivate a garden.

3—Joy-Bringer in the ART of Living.

3 Names—ETHEL BARRYMORE $(5 + 7 = 12$ **(3)**— Stage and Screen,
JOHN PHILIP SOUSA $(2 + 7 + 3 = 12$ **(3)**
Band (3) leader.
EDISON (3) who developed use of *Electricity* (3).

3 Birth—*Robert Edmund Jones* Sagit.   Dec. 12 1887
Noted colorful $12 = 3$ 3   24
Stage designer.   9 $+$ 6 $+$ 6
[60] $= 21 =$ **(3)**.

Vocation—Activity requiring accuracy, regularity, endurance, punctuality, mastery of detail, and concentration on work in hand.

Professions—Army officer, musical director, designer or manufacturer of musical instruments, patterns or fine tools. Architect, engraver, draftsman, mechanical engineer, bridge builder. Actuary, accountant, efficiency expert, train dispatcher. Text book or fiction writer, playwright, drama critic. Stage manager, theatrical producer. Surgeon, diagnostician, osteopath, chiropodist, biologist, physicist. Statistician, librarian, economist, college professor, designer or director of political "machinery."

Business—Banker, renting agent, manager or buyer—store, department, office or factory, where one must be critic of materials, workmanship or schedules. Manufacturer, dealer or technician in steel or building trades, hardware, plumbing, coal, furniture, factory or office equipment. Credit-man, bookkeeper, cashier, stenographer, secretary, proof-reader, linotype operator, filing expert. Printer, book-binder, weaver, tailor. Bank or post office clerk, in army, mail, or civil service.

Avocation—Clay modeling, wood-carving, book-binding, making scrap-books. Building stone fences; designing bath rooms, furniture, time-saving devices for office, home, kitchen or workshop. Start a clipping service in the line of your special interest—information gathered will be of value to you—and to those whom it touches. Try your hand at fiction, or managing home theatricals.

4/4 March-time Military Rhythm

4 Names—Generals WASHINGTON, MacARTHUR.
EISENHOWER,
GEORGE WASHINGTON GOETHALS,
Builder Panama Canal
GEORGE EASTMAN (3 + 10 = 4), Kodak
manufacturer.

4 Birth—*Orville Wright* born in Leo Aug. 19 1871*

$$\frac{5 \quad 8}{4} + \frac{10 \quad 8}{9}$$

Inventor of
Airplane (4).
= 13 = (4)

* Add Year.

[61]

Vocation—Activity calling for frequent change, an investigative turn of mind, initiative, keen judgment of human nature, ability to sell, or handle the public—especially the opposite sex.

Professions—Government official, lawyer, politician, promoter, secret service agent. Theatrical producer, actor, dancer, composer. Writer, philosopher, editor, translator. Sales-Counselor, psychologist, character analyst, personnel director. Travel guide, photographer, retoucher. Exponent of physical culture or new methods of rejuvenation—plastic surgeon, masseur (or masseuse). Athletic coach, professional sportsman, tennis or golf player. Aviator, explorer, navigator, geographer. Surveyor, assayer, mining or civil engineer.

Business—Inventor of new or better methods. Salesman (or woman) in any field, especially tours, advertising, stocks, bonds, sport goods, rejuvenation methods, insurance, real estate, automobiles. Broker, trader, booking agent. Conductor, guide, ticket agent. Reporter, investigator, inspector, detective. Director employment, adjustment, or repair service. Furrier, cleaning and dyeing. In theatre, travel, mining, government or civil service.

Avocation—Selling tours to gain one for yourself. Promoting entertainment or athletic events; making masks. Take up some rejuvenation system—hiking, dancing, physical culture. Find new places to go. Invent new ways of doing things. Learn to analyze your friends, especially those of opposite sex, by some method of character analysis. Your natural flair in this line may enable you to start a placement service of your own.

The AUTOMOBILE SPEEDS LIFE in AMERICA.

5 *Names*—HENRY FORD (7 + 7 = 14 (5), inventor
  automobile (5).
  FRANK LLOYD WRIGHT (5 + 5 + 4 = 14
  (5) *architecture* (5).

5 *Birth*—*Frank Lloyd Wright*, born Gemini June 8 1869*
  with *Architecture* (5)   3   6   6
  in both Name and Birth.   9 + 5
     = 11 = (5)

* Add Year.

NUMBER 6—LET YOUR VOICE BE HEARD

Vocation—Activity which calls for the expression of the voice through art or kindly counsel, where social qualities combine with a sense of responsibility and a desire to raise existing standards.

Professions—Home-maker, for family, or college groups; professional hostess; director boy or girl scouts, student adviser, tutor, governess, professor. Librarian, preacher, lecturer, economist. Publisher, editor, writer, collaborator, translator. Dramatist, actor, costume designer. Poet, song writer, musician, singer, accompanist. Doctor, Osteopath, institutional head, nurse, bacteriologist, physicist, chemist, cosmetician. Organizer—lodge, educational or community projects. Civil, electrical or sanitary engineer.

Business—Publisher, book-seller. Merchant—Department store, home commodities, furniture, school supplies, electrical appliances. Home building contractor, electrician, in public utility service. Instructor in trade schools, arts and crafts. Interior decorator, weaver, book designer. Tailor, clothier, costumer, beauty expert. Secretary, cashier, hotel clerk. Manager institution, hospital, hotel, building, tea room, restaurant or club. Active in co-operative, labor or educational movements.

Avocation—Professional hostess, spokesman for a worthy cause; tutoring. Interior decorating, designing monograms, book covers, book-plates. Develop your voice, study dramatic art, pageantry. Assume responsibility in educational or community project, direct home talent plays. Write songs, poetry, or become a counselor on home and marriage problems.

      6—MUSICAL, EDUCATOR, or in SELLING,
           Your WORD carries Weight.

6 *Names*—ENRICO CARUSO (10 + 5 = 6), noted
      Opera tenor.
      BING CROSBY (5 + 10 = 6), singer, TV
      and Radio.
      SELLING (6)—MACY and WANAMAKER,
      merchants.

6 *Birth*—John Logie Baird,
         Leo Aug. 13 1888*
          5 + 8 + 4 + 7 = 24 = (6).
    Inventor of TV
         24 = 6.

* Add Year.

Vocation—Activity where Quality counts, where confidence and perseverance, finish and technique, ability to keep one's own counsel, and the confidence of others, establish a standard of authority and perfection.

Professions—Financier, investment counselor. Scientific authority, specialist, surgeon, oculist, psychiatrist, psycho-analyst. Physicist, geologist, archaeologist, metallurgist, mining engineer. Jurist, patent or real estate lawyer, preacher, teacher in professional or finishing school. Historian, editorial writer, satirist. Authority on etiquette, form, or religious rites. Violinist, organist, pianist, dramatist, actor, model, stylist. Designer of jewelry, stage settings, period furniture Architect, landscape artist. Naturalist, horticulturist. Taxidermist, sportsman.

Business—Should be in business for self or in authoritative capacity (no 50-50 partnerships). Real estate operator, appraiser or estimator. Farmer, stock or poultry raiser. Nurseryman, florist, tree surgeon, landscape gardener. Dealer in lumber, furniture, antiques, jewelry, sporting goods. Superintendent or craftsman in finishing trades—cabinet maker, watch maker, stage settings.

Avocation—Authority on antiques, historical settings, period furniture, jewelry, etiquette, form, or correct usage. Designing draperies or interiors. Adding the finishing touch in any field; professional packer. Cultivate out-door activities—sports, golf, country club, landscape gardening. Investigate psycho-analysis. Take up some phase of research in accord with personal hobby.

7—Have YOU the LINCOLN WIT and TENACITY?

7 *Names*—WILLIAM SHAKESPEARE (7 + 9 = 16 (7) writer for *Stage*.
GEORGE WASHINGTON (3 + 4 = 7), *Dignity* in *Government*.

7 *Birth*—Darwin taught *Evolution* (7), a *Revolution* (7) in Science. *Lincoln* (7) *freed* (11) the *slave* (5). Both born in Aquarius Feb. 12 1809

$$11 + \frac{2\ 3\ 9}{14 = 5} = (11-5) = 7.$$

[64]

Vocation—Activity calling for keen judgment of values, executive diplomacy, engineering tact, ability to organize and bring definite plans to completion. *Professions*—Senator, army officer. Judge, corporation lawyer. Bishop or church head. Political or financial adviser. Philosopher, poet, physicist. Osteopath, oculist. Engineer, executive, business analyst, inventor. Personnel director, merchandise counselor, buyer. Accountant, actuary, statistician. Theatrical producer, dramatist, actor. Critic, reviewer, cartoonist, editor, publisher. Librarian, compiler. School or college head; teacher manual training, athletic coach. Bandmaster, composer, orchestra leader. Sportsman, boxer, wrestler, swimmer, skater.

Business—Banker, broker, manufacturer. Executive—department store, factory, or in any phase of "big business." Purchasing agent, buyer in any field, from cattle to advertising. Paymaster, employment or office manager. Law clerk, collector, renting or booking agent. Contractor, builder, skilled craftsman, master mechanic. Dealer in lumber, furniture, factory or office equipment; group insurance, books, lodge supplies. Importer, shipper; commission merchant. Chef, cook, manager restaurant chain. Police official, in city or mail service.

Avocation—Patron of the Arts. Organizer or manager of club affairs, dramatics; ball team. Take up some form of athletics—fencing, boxing, swimming. Accept seat on a board of directors. Be a professional shopper. Inform yourself on law of contracts for self protection. Study philosophy. Invent something.

8—CREATOR—EDITOR—BUILDER

8 Names—GEORGE BERNARD SHAW (3 + 8 + 6 — 17 (8), playwright.

HEARST (8) Newspaper Chain (8).

VANDERBILT (8) Financial interests.

8 Birth—Wm. Randolph Hearst Sr.

$$\begin{array}{lll} & \text{Taurus Apr. 29 1863} \\ \text{Vincent Astor, Financier,} & 2 \quad 4 & 18 \\ \text{Scorpio Nov. 15 1891} & \overline{6 + 11 + 9} \\ \qquad\qquad 6 \quad 10 & \overline{(6\text{-}11)} = 8. \\ \quad 8 + 11 + \overline{7} = (11\text{-}6) = 8. \end{array}$$

Vocation—Activity calling for happy expression of talent in broad, free way; where artistry combines with personality, understanding, and the large view.

Professions—Singer, actor, entertainer, dancer, musician, poet. Portrait artist, designer, illustrator. Writer, humorist, newspaper correspondent. Publisher, educator, lecturer; astronomer. Lawyer, banker, preacher. Healer, doctor, oculist, chemist, pharmacist, head of sanitarium or health resort. Railroad official. Publicity man, promoter of tours, benefits, large entertainment ventures. Navigator, aviator, forester. Professional ball player. Social service expert.

Business—Broker, trader. Oil promoter, or manager chain of oil stations. Publicity or circulation manager, reporter, newspaper man. Router of traffic or freight. Railway mail clerk, conductor, ranger, skipper. Salesman or dealer—entertainment, travel or health service, art goods, beauty aids, millinery, furs, advertising, or decorative novelties. Hair or beauty specialist; visiting nurse. Illumination expert in amusement resorts, theatre, or window display. Window trimmer, display technician.

Avocation—Philanthropist; hostess to traveling celebrities, free lance feature writer. Look up points of law for personal or professional benefit. Obtain trip by selling tours. Study dancing, voice or dramatics. Invent new means of cheer for hospitals or institutions. Evolve some new kind of Health candy and then find ways to advertise it.

9—HEALTH, LOVE, MONEY in SERVICE to PUBLIC.

9 *Names*—Noted MAYO (**9**) Clinic at Rochester, N. Y.

      GRACE KELLY (7 + 2 = **9**),

      CLARK GABLE, Movies.

      Chas. GOODYEAR, inventor vulcanized rubber.

9 *Birth*—*Ralph Waldo*

      Emerson Gemini May 25 1803

      Writer· $3 + 5 + 7 + 3 = 18 = (9)$

      Philosopher   9

Vocation—Activity calling for quick insight, penetration, decision, a stimulating personality and capacity for leadership.

Professions—President, Congressman, inspirational leader in promotion of new enterprises. Inventor, explorer; director of advertising or publicity; political campaigner. Lawyer, jurist; member of Intelligence service. Lecturer, evangelist, preacher, psychologist, psycho-analyst, philosopher who needs a definite system of deduction, such as graphology or numbers, as a "seive for his psychic." Musician, musical director, composer, critic. Dancer, entertainer, magician. Artist on radio or stage; movie actor. Poet, painter, sculptor. Biographer, novelist; character analyst.

Business—Postmaster, Revenue Collector, in government, mail, or detective service. Promoter or organizer of co-operative movements. Radio announcer or program builder. Advertising solicitor. Telegraph or telephone operator. Movie camera man. Insurance adjuster. Auctioneer. Booking or ticket agent. Beauty specialist; masseur (masseuse). Manager of music store; entertainment or transportation service; wholesale shoe, dress or paper house.

Avocation—Horse back riding, attending the races. Develop your musical or dramatic talent. Promote some friend or new movement. Make it your business and pleasure to meet important people, collect their autographs and absorb the atmosphere of the limelight. Be a magician now and then; evolve marionettes or create advertising posters. Listen to your "hunch."

11—Born for ADVENTURE. a LIGHT in Your World!

11 Names—Herbert HOOVER. former President, economist.

J. Edgar HOOVER. Director of the F.B.I.

Ed SULLIVAN, noted Columnist.

11 Birth—*Andrew Taylor Still* Leo Aug. 6 1828*

Founder Osteopathy   5   8   10

New *Light on Health.* $\overline{4\ +\ 7}$ = $\overline{(11)}$

* Add Year.

NUMBER 22—THE MASTER BUILDER

Vocation—Activity calling for organization, skillful understanding of human nature, ability to blend opposing views, build a large plan and realize its accomplishment.

Professions—Statesman, diplomat, dictator, chief of Secret Service. Army or Navy officer; explorer. International financier, law or trade expert. Economist, physicist. Organizer or director of political machinery, world tours, co-operative movements, professional ball teams, racing meets, athletics, or large public ventures. Racer, aviator. Fiction or sports writer. "Master of rules," be it foot-ball, bridge, or ritual. Professional bridge player. Theatrical producer, orchestra leader, dramatist, actor. Critic, translator. Character analyst, vocational expert, psycho-analyst, psychiatrist, Osteopath; director of Reconstruction activities, for soldiers or other groups. Actuary, C. P. A. Architect; bridge-builder. Estimator of values, of far reaching import.

Business—Organizer or director of labor, co-operative, group or chain enterprises. Manufacturer on large scale. Exporter, shipper, foreign buyer. Executive in steamship lines. Factory or business supervisor. Bank inspector, efficiency expert, master mechanic. Accountant, collector, legal secretary. Stage manager, booking agent.

Avocation—Building or deciphering codes. Organizing groups for exploring some new vicinity. Playing politics; putting on theatricals. Study a Baedecker in prospect of a trip abroad. Try your hand in pottery, soap sculpture, basketry, block printing. Play tennis, or fence. Make it a game with yourself to get things done with greater speed.

22—GLOBAL—STATESMAN—MASTER MIND

22 Names—Richard E. BYRD, Arctic, Antarctic Explorer.

RICHARD MILHAUS NIXON, Vice-Pres.

$$(7 + 11 + 4 = 22)$$

ALBERT Bradley (22-4) Board Chairman, General Motors, largest corporation in the world.

22 Birth—*John D. Rockefeller*

Capitalist

Cancer July 8, 1839*

$$4 + 7 + 8 + 3 = (22)$$

* Add Year.

[68]

PART II

Character Grams

CHAROMANCY—An Answer to Your Query.
Reading the Subconscious Mind.

EIGHT SLANTS ON YOUR GOOD NATURE

WHAT'S IN A NAME?

IDIOSYNCRASIES

HOW TO REACH YOUR HEART OR POCKET BOOK

CHARACTER SKETCHING

YOUR WHEEL OF FORTUNE
This Year's Adventure for You.
List of Countries, States, Cities.

CHARACTER TRAITS—VOCATIONS—PASTIMES
Music, Colors, Foods, Gems, Flowers according to word value.

RULES for PLAYING

For Two or more:
Each player draws a Letter-Number from the lot of Character Grams cut from last pages. One holding highest Number is entitled to information first. One with lowest becomes "Guardian and Revealer of Secrets" who unfolds to seeker from chapters that follow, an answer to his query and hidden truths regarding his dual nature, based on:

BIRTHDATE (Inner) and NAME (Outer self)

WRITE FULL BIRTH NAME. From Number-Key, opposite page, Place above each Vowel (a-e-i-o-u-, y when sounded as "i") its number value. Add double numbers to single digit, as 1 3 4, except the master 11 and 22 which stand intact

Add Vowels of each Name, then altogether for full total.

$$\frac{15 = 6}{5 \quad 1 \quad 9} \quad + \quad \frac{10 = 16(7)}{1 \qquad 9}$$ SOUL -*Courage* (7)
Talent- *Printer* (10)

Benjamin   Franklin
2 5 1 4 5   6 9 5 2 3 5

$$\frac{17}{8} \qquad + \qquad \frac{30}{3} = (11)$$ PERSONALITY -*Auth-*
2 5 5 1 1 4 9 5   6 9 1 5 2 3 9 5   *ority- Independent*

$$\frac{32}{5} \qquad + \qquad \frac{40}{4} = (9)$$ MIND -DESTINY--A
World figure in *Pub-*

Born Capricorn January 17 1706   *lic* Relations.

$$10 \quad + \quad \frac{1 \quad 8 \quad 14}{9} \quad + \quad 5 = 24 \ (6)$$ SPIRIT

Pioneer   Diplomat   Invention   *Journalist, Edu-*
cator, whose WORD still rings true.

MEANING of any Number (Positive or Reverse) may be found in words adding to such Number, as brief examples pp. 118-121.

	See also	Pages
VOWELS -	Heart or Desire	-98 -102
CONSONANTS -	Personality-	78 -87
Individual and FULL NAME -		78 -87

Present Name shows one's present power and environment.

BIRTH Numbers and NATAL SIGN- 55 -68.

Chapter I

CHAROMANCY

Reading the Subconscious Mind

An Answer to Your Query "What Shall I Do?"

Let your Inner Self Decide.

Guardian and Revealer of Secrets (see previous page) places the Seeker opposite him and directs him thus:

Guardian: "Ask the question in your mind 'What Shall I Do?' regarding a certain thing. Be careful not to think of two ways at once as your subconscious can only work on One thing at a time. Make the picture clear and sharp, as you would *like to have it*. Now give me quickly from your agile mind, four letters of the alphabet."

Guardian takes these four letters from pack of Character Grams and places them in front of him in the order given, adding their number values, as shown below, to find the final total.

A B C D E F G H I   J K L M N O P Q R
1 2 3 4 5 6 7 8 9   1 2 3 4 5 6 7 8 9

S T U V W X Y Z
1 2 3 4 5 6 7 8

Each letter-number is read separately, in the order given, from the list which follows, and then the final total. With a little practice you will be able to weave a smooth statement of what the numbers reveal.

Supposing the Seeker said F E C D,
$$6 + 5 + 3 + 4 = 18.$$
you would interpret thus:

6—You should gain some added knowledge. Talk it over with some one before you proceed.

[71]

5—Go some place. Investigate. Be willing to change or alter your plans, if need be. Deal with the opposite sex. Your answer may come through them, if you understand them.

3—Be friendly. It might be well to write a letter. Blending the three numbers thus far, we have: Through discussion (6) with the opposite sex (5) in a friendly (3) way, you should be able to develop

4—A Definite plan—but scheme, count the cost, before you

18—Complete your plans or close the transaction. Cooperation with someone else should bring a successful outcome, although you may go on some trip to accomplish it.

If the Seeker desires to know what is in another's mind, Guardian must ask him to describe the person very definitely, as to size, color of the eyes, hair, and how he was dressed when he saw him last. Be serious, and ask sufficient questions to obtain an accurate description. Then when you see that the Seeker has a definite picture of the person in his own mind, ask him for four letters, quickly. Now read these after the manner suggested above. This gives an interpretation of the other person's subconscious mind, through the mind of the Seeker.

1. Decide. Be receptive to a New Idea. Listen to your Intuition. Welcome a new environment.

2. Analyze both sides of the situation. Gather further facts or materials. Consider the wish or rights of another. Study him. Bring two ideas, or people together harmoniously.

3. Be Friendly, sociable, entertaining. Look your best. Write a letter. Make someone happy, and you will be surprised with a happy return.

4. A definite plan. Scheme. Count the cost. Save your money. Keep busy.

5. Go some place. Investigate. Be willing to change or alter your plans, if need be. Deal with the opposite sex—your answer may come through them, if you understand them. (If you have anything you wish to sell, the number before and after 5 should show / to handle it.)

6. Talk it over. Gain added knowledge. Let your voice be heard, tactfully. Render a service. Responsibility graciously assumed may open up the way.

7. Stop! Look! Listen! Finish what you have started in the most perfect way possible. Keep the idea or plan under cover. Go to the country, or to a quiet spot where you may be alone, and let your intuition come through to give you the right course of action to follow. Appear at your best. Silence is better, but if necessary to speak, do so in a dignified, authoritative way.

8. Build and organize your plan. Engineer it through, tactfully. Work with others diplomatically. Success, financially or otherwise, rests upon your good judgment in values, whether it be buying materials or service, or arranging your time to count for the most.

9. Radiate. Love yourself and everyone in your world. Take a trip if you can—if this be physically impossible, then in your imagination. (As total: A happy completion of plans and expression of your talents in a larger way.)

10. See Number 1.

11. Decide quickly. Inspiration through a new beginning. Listen to your Intuition. Contact important people. Advertise your good qualities or plans by bringing them into the limelight in some way.

12. A Letter. Completion of your picture or plans in a happy way. Be an inventor of new ways to entertain, or carry out your special plan. You have the power within yourself to do it.

13. Good fortune, when you lay a careful plan, and then carry it out on time. Count the cost. Its success lies in the originality of design, and as much variety, color, and individuality as can be injected into something which must stand the test of time, and serve a definite purpose.

14. Improvement through change of method, schedule, or location. Investigate ways of doing the same thing in less time, or getting better results at less cost.

15. Discuss things with some member of the opposite sex. Improve your home atmosphere. Go some place where you may gain some added knowledge, and you will feel rejuvenated.

[73]

16. Technical obstacles may cause delay but recognition comes from quality in the end. Complete your part just the same. Be dignified and reserved. Speak with authority, but keep your own counsel until further developments occur.

You may have an idea you wish to talk over, which has been kept under cover for some time. It might be well to wait another day—*listen, you may uncover something* further if you draw out the other person. Keep the reins in your own hands.

17. Finish things quietly but in the best manner and you should enjoy a fair and just return. Then go to the country and think over a larger plan. Cooperate tactfully, but keep your own counsel.

18. Complete your plans. Close business transaction, through tactful co-operation with someone else. The outcome should be successful, though you may have to go on a long journey to accomplish it.

19. Starting one thing and finishing another, don't become confused. Stand still. Throw an atmosphere of love first around yourself, knowing that your right motive, when fulfilled, will benefit others too. This makes you a center of gravity to attract your own. Then radiate love to every one, and the thing or person you need should come running toward you. Take a trip, if you can. This should help to close the old cycle and start the new in a clear way.

20. Cooperate and be willing to share the honors with someone else. Don't bluff. Analyze, and then put things together smoothly or tactfully.

21. Happiness through having brought things to completion. Recognition of your ability as an entertainer. You and another person of the opposite sex should have a happy social time.

22. Definite plan on a large scale. Deal with the most important people. Work through groups. Be the diplomat, play politics. Take the longest trip possible. Foreign contacts would be of benefit. At least gain a broad view. Gamble safely with any plan by first carefully counting the cost. Do the big thing yet keep your balance. Do not become extravagant and overreach the mark.

23. Go on a short trip. Have a genial chat with the opposite sex. If you have anything you desire to sell, present it to two people socially.

24. Study to improve your plan. Talk it over with someone and work out a schedule together. Analyze the cost. The right system, carried out on time, with order in home and surroundings should establish you and your service.

25. Seek out some member of the opposite sex to help you investigate or uncover that which is needed to complete and perfect your plan. A short trip to the country, or a quiet spot might be of aid. (If Seeker be a woman, and single) : There is an excellent indication of a marriage proposal for you if you handle the opposite sex tactfully. Call attention to his fine points, keep your own counsel and quietly uncover his views.

26. Organize your plans. Engineer them through with diplomacy. See that everything is in perfect order. Speak convincingly before any group. A service based on system should bring good financial return and enable you to buy, build, plan for a home or a larger undertaking. You should be able to assume easily any responsibility for another.

27. You have two things to finish. Polish both of them until their finished aspect radiates Quality. A trip to the country or a quiet atmosphere might aid. Draw out the other person through the radiation of good-will. Let go, and you may uncover things of value to you.

28. A little more data, well-organized, will help you build your idea into more definite form. Systematize your time. Use your good brain to work out the right financial backing for your plan. Then contact an 8 to help you put it over.

29. Occupy the limelight·graciously, expressing your talents generously for the benefit of friend or group. Advertise but be willing to share honors with another. Radiate good will.

30. A letter, or happy social time. Play with the children. See Number 3.

31. A plan carried through with design, a social con-

tact well planned, or an artistic idea expressed with excellent sense of proportion and line.

32. Improvement, investigation, or change, through diplomatic, social contact with opposite sex. Be alert, adaptable. A short trip should benefit.

33. Be a host (or hostess) to friends, children, artists, writers, or those who need your cheery atmosphere. Present music, food, and entertainment in a colorful way. Discuss projects pertaining to children, artists, education, literary effort, or the social life in your community.

34. Finish things happily in an orderly way. See a lawyer who is an old friend before you sign any papers. Plan a happy occasion for the family in the country.

35. Success through managing any group where both sexes combine business with pleasure. Good financial return should come to you through selling something you have written, or by acting as manager for any social or athletic affair. Put your plan over with a genial sense of humor. Carry it out by correspondence if impossible to do so in person.

Chapter II

EIGHT SLANTS ON YOUR GOOD NATURE WITH CHARACTER GRAMS

Follow Rules for Playing given on page seventy.
Guardian and Revealer of Secrets reads paragraph in each chapter which deals with the Number found in the Name.

1—YOUR TYPE OF MIND—Number of *Full Birth Name* under *What's In a Name*, present Chapter.

2—*HEREDITARY TRAITS—*Number of Last Name at birth,* see present chapter.

3—INDIVIDUALITY—Number of *First Name*, or that by which one is most frequently called, see present chapter.

4—IDIOSYNCRASIES—Count *Number of letters* in full birth name. See Part II, Chapter III.

5—MISSING NOTES—Are all nine digits present in full birth name? Find Numbers Missing, in Part II, Chapter IV.

6—HOW TO TOUCH YOUR HEART OR POCKET BOOK—See *First Vowel* in name most frequently used, Part II, Chapter V.

7—PRESENT ACTIVITIES AND POSSIBILITIES in total of *present signature*. Read this Number under *What's in a Name?* Present chapter.

8—YOU! Sketched by your friends. See directions in Part II, Chapter VI.

As Guardian proceeds to reveal the Secrets, if the interpretation ring true, he should be supported by the

---

* Traits inherited from mother are seen in her last name before marriage.

YEAS of those sitting in council—if they miss the mark, utter silence should reign.

WHAT'S IN A NAME?

Destiny and Type of Mind—in Full Birth Name.
Inherited traits—in Last Name at birth.
Individuality expressed through First and Given Names.
Present Activities and Possibilities in present signature.

As the actuary of an insurance company bases his findings upon the *law of averages*; as the doctor relies upon the same law in symptom and remedy, so are the comments which follow, based upon the application of a definite rule to thousands of cases, handled over a period of years, dealing with the individual and his problem.

No one is a pure ONE, TWO, THREE, or any other number—he is a combination of several. By an understanding of all the varied shadings of his nature he may arrange his own life mosaic to better meet the demands of his Birthpath Urge, and find that peace within which brings success without.

Your Name,—your point of contact with the world, should be in rhythm or harmony with your total birthpath Number,—as high or higher in value, and Odd or Even, as the case may be. One exception to this rule is 5 and 8; do-sol-do, or 1-5-8 are the three strong notes in the octave. 8 is the one number which can hold the variable 5 in its proper place.

ONE NAME

Original enough to be different without being odd; rebelling at command yet responsive to persuasion; winning in the end by conforming for the moment, you have a style and a mind all your own.

One being a part of every number, you should be a better judge of human nature than the average individual. But if you have known disappointment through taking the advice of another, you have reaped your reward—you have come to lead, not to follow.

Having decided upon your goal, do not make too many curves or detours to please a friend or pamper your own

[78]

fancy. If you swerve from the path you may lose the road and have to begin all over again.

A new idea for you may provide a greater thrill than money in the bank, but see that you take action quickly—before another claims your mind. An idea-producer for others in every station of life, why not associate with the 7's, 8's, or 22's and obtain a due reward for your effort? Friends among the 3's, 5's, and 9's will bring you color and social life, and a chance to express your creative urge in some artistic way, but don't let others absorb you. Intelligent variety is a stimulant for you, but would you kindle the flame and flee? With you, one must step lively and have a keen intellect to be intriguing.

Whatever your problems may be, you have that initiative and intuition which should enable you to solve them, if you stand still long enough to let the idea come through. But don't expose your plans to the cold air of private or public opinion. They will grow for *you*, but not for others—so keep them under your own personal eye.

The particular field in which your creative talent may find its most happy expression may be seen in the other numbers in your Name or Birth Path.

You are here to win—see that you don't get lazy and let procrastination steal your time away. Living fearlessly, One day at a time, forever on the edge of a precipice without falling over, knowing that at the last moment something will save the day, you are bound to have that richness of adventure the staid and sure will never know. But when the next turn in the road looms before you, stop a moment and listen. . . .

Anticipating the other person's next move, anticipating the need in any field and supplying it—there lies your happiness and great good fortune.

Young you will always be, by reason of *another new idea*.

TWO NAME

Greater recognition for your good qualities lies in boosting "the other fellow." One, like the eagle, may soar alone, but for you, companionship is essential. Imitative.

[79]

analytical, with an appreciation of music, and perhaps (though your friends may not know it) interested in the occult, you are a combination of qualities—which makes for your charm. One never knows which will be uppermost.

Unassuming, pleasing, dressed in good taste in the prevailing style, you are an example of good form and perfect grooming. Other Two's whom you may not find this way are on the *reverse* side of their wheel. They should not forget that *sometimes* the "clothes make the man."

With your great desire for peace and harmony, you may at times remain the power behind the throne, giving up your personal desires for the sake of others, or delaying your own pleasure until a later date.

Because of your sensitivity and desire for approbation you may hesitate to put your best foot forward until you are sure of your ground. Analyze every situation; gather all the knowledge to be had on your most important venture, then proceed diplomatically to win your way. You could be a professional collector or statistician in whatever field your chief interest lies.

You may not know it, but you have that hypnotic power which can bring others around to your way of thinking—if you do not criticize or call attention to another's shortcomings. Concede for the moment that his idea is right, just as it stands, and build up *from it* to your own.

Patience with your own affairs will give you somewhat more patience with others. No matter how individualistic you may be, your greater happiness and success lies in associating harmoniously with others, functioning through groups rather than as an individual.

You can handle *Two* or more things, or people, at one time. As an adjuster of differences, or as a diplomatic go-between, you have power to bring peace and harmony in your realm. Upon your system and tact depends the smooth running of your affairs.

If you have not yet found your life mate, begin to study human nature. The best way to win and hold any member of the opposite sex is by *understanding* him.

Peace be with you.

[80]

THREE NAME

You should be the life of the party and have a host of friends, as your sense of humor was well developed when you were born. You may love a home and children, but don't wear your heart on your sleeve. You are the easy-going type that may encourage others to take advantage of your good nature if you are not alert.

Friendly, sympathetic, a genial host and splendid judge of foods, you will keep your youth much longer than those with purely adult interests. A little greater control over your emotions, making your head rule your heart, and purse strings, may be of benefit to both.

Dancing, Color, Rhythm, make for happiness with you, yet you in turn have come to be a joy-bringer to others, and can be an excellent entertainer. Literary or artistic, there are many delightful avenues for the expression of your imaginative and creative talent.

Be careful not to criticize—let each one learn his own lesson. If a Three become too analytical he is apt to have a tinge of rheumatism now and then, and this might spoil your otherwise joyful plans.

Dress in the lighter shades. Make your sense of humor and your charm count, attracting those friends who are just a bit beyond you at the present moment.

At your leisure read *The Way Out* for Three, Part I, Chapter IV. Make *three* people smile each day and watch the comments on your own increasing beauty.

Yours for a happy morrow!

FOUR NAME

You have a keen, analytical, logical mind, and keep busy, mentally and physically. Energetic, systematic, and punctual, you expect others to be the same.

Try not to measure everyone by your own rule. Remember that the majority of people have not been blessed with your keen eye for accuracy and proportion. Don't be so conscientious about your work that you are annoyed by those who loaf on the job.

With a 4 total name coming from 3 and 1, you are creative and artistic, and can build your own plans into definite form. With a 4 total coming from 2 and 2, you can tear things apart and put them together again, and be an excellent builder of system and efficiency. Organize your own time to make it count for the most, but don't lose a chance for a hearty laugh.

If you have been so occupied that your sense of humor has not had the attention it deserves, it is not too late to develop it now. Too much economy of sentiment may not attract the friends who should bring you good cheer. Your love nature is not a changeable one, yet you are apt to be too busy to give it much attention. Fair play works both ways, you know.

Conscientious and thrifty, you know how to drive a good bargain. You believe in saving your money and feel that a like policy would be wisdom for all. Why not spend an hour with a Five? He will give you that added boost to put your pet plan over whether you agree with him or not. Each Number meets his greatest test in the one "next door." Get acquainted with your neighbor.

FIVE NAME

Amiable, adaptable, an Eternal Question Mark, you are a personality stimulant, worth while! You can be the life of the party, but if things move too slowly, you may take in several affairs in one evening.

Variety and change are the spice of life with you. Your love of short trips may even include the marriage license bureau. Five appreciates the opposite sex until he finds them necessary, then in his insatiable desire for freedom he is apt to oppose their assistance, and run away from his Opportunity only to meet another's Opportunity on the way.

Others should recognize your inherent love of freedom. You cannot be held by force, but given plenty of rope, you may wander, surprising us with your early return! One should urge you to *go*, if he desires you to stay!

You keep things moving! Whatever may be the situation, you have the power to figure a better way. You are a life buoy to the *even* Numbers, though you may be here today and gone tomorrow. Should any of your less wise friends insist that "a rolling stone gathers no moss," you may reply, "True, but it acquires considerable polish just the same."

Keep on *rolling* till you meet someone who can keep you guessing, and so hold your interest. Having thus met your Waterloo, you will graduate to 6 and proceed to tell the rest of us how to find our mate and hold him, too. Yours for a new thrill tomorrow!

SIX NAME

One of your first keys to happiness is a real home atmosphere. Married or single, head of a country estate or living in a single room, you have the ability to establish that homey atmosphere which makes for friends and hospitality.

A second key to your enjoyment lies in having someone for whom you feel responsible. A born adviser, you need at least an audience of one (the more the better), to whom you may express your views on matters of importance.

Responsibility is necessary for your happiness and success, but do not allow yourself to become unduly worried over trifles or allow fatigue to undermine your health by doing for others what they should do for themselves.

An excellent conversationalist, you may enjoy crossing intellectual swords, and should carry your point over your keenest adversary by the logic of your reasoning and your true knowledge of affairs.

A too fluent Six may annoy his neighbor. You must know when to stop, if you really wish to be heard. However, cultivate your voice still further—you may be called upon to speak or take part in some musical or dramatic program in the not distant future. Your natural understanding in matters of health, coupled with your desire to assist others, should make you a valuable asset in any community betterment program.

Learn to decide quickly—that will lift you to the next rung of your ladder. Cultivate a hobby—fall in Love—with *yourself*, and watch new love flow toward you. Success to you—the world's Big Brother (or Sister)!

[83]

You desire the best or none at all. As a stately pine tree, more dignified than the rest, you have come to occupy the stage and be the final word in your world.

Sensitive to atmosphere and personalities, you may hide your real feelings by apparent indifference. You dislike to mingle with the common crowd. Unless the occasion be worthy, you prefer an hour with your favorite book, or you may hie yourself to the country to escape weekend guests.

Gracious and affable, or rivaling the Sphinx in your silence, your first reaction to any new plan is apt to be No—yet if one retire gracefully, you may later respond in your own good time, with an improved idea of your own. You do not move easily, either by command or persuasion, yet once your opinion is asked, with the right approach—you speak with authority, you know your ground.

You carry that air which bids one stay at a respectful distance, yet feel especially flattered when you really unbend and take him into your confidence. Keeping well your own counsel, you may not always be understood, yet in you lies a wealth of hidden gold, if one have the patience to uncover it.

Appreciating appreciation, whether you admit it or not, if others seem ungrateful, ask yourself, "Am I withholding a fair amount of 'praise-tonic' from them?" Think it over. Let go. Don't nurse a pet peeve—ever! Snap out of it. Seek an Eight—he'll put your plan over on a larger scale, and you'll soon be leaving the past behind you, going over the top with greater material success because of your real technique and quality.

Finish what you start, but be willing to move on. You have still larger worlds to conquer.

EIGHT NAME

A born manager, you can keep several people busy and happy at the same time, if you exercise the engineering diplomacy at your command. While in your well-meant zeal some may consider you a driver, you are usually a tactful one, able to win the support of those worthwhile, to your definite and well-laid plan. You admire fair play, and are willing to pay a fair compensation to those who are able to deliver the goods on time.

Flattery does not sway the true Eight, nor does emotional display—hence one had better sharpen his wits if he expects to engage you in an encounter. While you may disagree, you hold no grudge. It is only a negative Eight who feels he has been unfairly treated. Holding your own emotions in check with your well-balanced intellect, you help others to do the same.

With a good memory for names and faces, as an editor, executive, or excellent manager anywhere, passing judgment upon the rest of us, you are the transformer of Ideas into concrete realities.

With politeness as your social insurance policy, and diplomacy your business builder, you should enjoy more happiness and success married than single. A large spacious home where you may be a gracious host should be a good professional, as well as a personal asset, and lead you into the love vibration of Nine where romance and travel await you.

May success attend you and speed you on your way!

NINE NAME

You are a radiant sun in your world, whose warming rays have the power to make those about you grow and bloom. Why? Because Nine includes all the other numbers. With their experiences you are already familiar.

Your magnetism, reaching farther, brings a greater reaction than that of a less vital or important person. Hence be careful, criticise not. Your words are your boomerang. For you, goodwill toward all is most important. You can afford to overlook the little things that annoy the lesser Numbers. They cannot possibly hurt you unless you lower yourself to their level.

Whatever you desire, build your picture clear and then travel toward it. If the way be impeded physically, go in your imagination, just the same. The more of the world you see the better, but until you are free to roam, understanding human nature right where you are will open the door to larger freedom.

Kindly as you are, don't give everything away or be too generous with your sympathy. Help others, show them the law, but do not try to demonstrate it for them. Learn to look out a little more for "Number One," for in 10, you find your own Kingdom of Attainment.

You cannot pull the whole world into heaven with you. Just know that the deserving will find their heaven too, as you have found yours—health, love, money, by reason of the large service you have rendered.

> *"Laugh and the world laughs with you;*
> *Weep and you weep alone."*

The world is yours and everything in it, according to the radiance of your own shining.

We love you and hope you will continue to love us in return.

ELEVEN NAME

You are here to *shine,* and be such a radiant light that all the world takes on a brighter hue. Your dynamic power, your intuitive penetration into the farthest corner, and your ability to make decisions quickly endow you with leadership in various fields.

But do not expect the impossible! On top of a Four-story building one cannot enjoy the same view as that afforded from an Eleven. No more can you expect the lesser Numbers who have not your *extended vision* to see as you do. Learn to lead the other *up gradually* to your point of view. Start from where he is, rather than from where you are, if you wish to win and hold his support or affection.

Music and contact with stimulating minds will keep your own highly-strung nervous system happy—see that you live up high, where you have plenty of air, and if possible, a view of the water.

Be careful in your associations—mingle with those worth while. Should you take the advice of other, less enlightened minds, you not only lose your own light but they too remain in darkness. Waver not. If you do, your own power is broken. Better to make a mistake and correct it, than be lost in a sea of doubt.

You have come to be an inspiration, and to help others in their shining too—you are a natural born advertiser. The radio, the movies, and all other avenues which may carry your message are light-bearers for you.

You are the stimulant we need! While we may not follow your pace, without *you* there would be no race.

We appreciate the honor of greeting the Winner!

TWENTY-TWO NAME

You are one who has the power to make or break yourself or others. Your highly developed intuition, your keen power of reasoning, and your ability to estimate the cost and then anticipate that give you an urge to try your speed and skill in winning, in every phase of life.

Your success lies in co-operating, co-ordinating, bringing together people or things into a happier and better organized whole. With your tact and diplomacy you can be politic without being a politician—yet you excel even there. Not so long ago, at the same election, there were three Ruths (22) elected to seats of prominence in Washington, while Albert, David, and Thomas (22) are not far behind.

Contact with groups is important for you; travel across the water if you can. You need a broad view and wide interests to provide a normal outlet for your high-powered current of energy. But, if instead of undertaking larger duties, you choose to hide your light under a bushel, your 22 will become a 4 and you will find yourself bound by detail and routine.

You should be a master analyst in any field, especially in the realm of human nature. You know how to tear apart, or psychoanalyze more painlessly than the other numbers. Be generous, but not too much so. Do not be too extravagant and suddenly find yourself a 4. Limitation for you is only to push you up and out into a larger field. Therefore hitch your wagon to a star, grasp the hand of a 1, who will carry you far—toward your next adventure.

May your own Good Fortune attend you!

[87]

Chapter III

IDIOSYNCRASIES

REVEALED BY NUMBER OF LETTERS IN FULL BIRTH NAME

The key to a door unlocks it and gives you access to the room. So will the number of letters in your name give us a key to that inner room of your own mind which is opened only on special occasions.

If in the business world you sign only your initials, the 1-2-3 shown below, apply there.

1 You have your own idea as to how things should be done, and may reverse the recognized order of the day just to be different. Suggestions should be given cautiously. Independent, yet sensitive, guard your own plans carefully. It is when you try to get others to see *your* point of view, which is far in advance of theirs, that they consider you odd. Variety is good for you—look up a stimulating 11, and together you should be able to start something that will really startle the natives.

2 Only two initials indicate a love of music, and a desire for cooperation, but it makes you too analytical, always weighing one thing against another, or tearing plans apart, so that you may not get them together again without working overtime. Take things a little easier. Add another letter, or drop 1 and you'll banish two bugaboos, indecision and delay. With Three letters, you'll have more time to play, and more ideas too, and that will help Two ways, you see.

3 A friendly, good-natured sort, who knows how to laugh in the face of trouble better than any other number, you might be loved into hell, but never

[88]

driven into heaven. Don't let any fear overtake you. Vivacious and artistic, you will always be youthful, able to make friends, and invent *some* way out. If you find the hostess drafting you into pantry duty to put the finishing touches on a salad or dessert, blame it on the Three.

4. You like to keep busy. No flights of fancy for you. Even if people did call you materialistic, that would not stop you from continuing to scheme and plan. You can't quite approve of people sitting around and resting. You feel they should have something more definite to do, and they will have, if they stay around you. You are an inspired hustler. We wouldn't be surprised if you were a shark in mathematics, but don't figure too closely either in pleasures for yourself or in compliments to others. Seek out some interesting member of the opposite sex, and let him initiate you into the thrills of a Five.

5 Free as the air, brisk and bustling, with a nose for news, don't let your spirit of investigation cause people to mistake your interest. You are a real rejuvenator and most people need that. In your struggle to make your head rule your emotions, sometimes the head wins. While to some your adventures appear foolhardy, in your own eyes you are a real explorer. Magnetic and a shrewd judge of character, you can imbue a comrade with new hope, even if some do consider you an exponent of the easy life. You may rise to power by devious ways, yet worry not, if you own no automobile. Walking is good for you!

6 You love a home and will make yourself at home no matter where you are; in fact you can fit in so well and assume responsibility so easily that you may be asked to come again. A born adviser, you should be a professional counselor and not waste your knowledge on those who may not appreciate its worth. Dramatic, your power of speech can put wind in another's sails, or take it out. But beware, your words, like chickens, come home to roost. Be a booster. You are the foundation on which our home and community rest.

7 What have you hidden away that still remains a secret? A greater reward awaits you when you bring out your hidden talents. Don't save things too long, nor be too serious. Once you start, tell it all, not just half of it. You like to keep something up your sleeve besides your elbow. Your hunch is O. K. but act on it. Don't spend so much time alone that you will be classed as a mystery. In a quiet nook, a book, or a blonde may hold your attention, if with dignity and decorum she knows how to keep silence and lets the atmosphere be punctuated only by your droll wit. You are a gold mine for some one, but who will it be?

8 You have the magic power that can transform enemies into friends, ideas into plans, plans into tangible results measured in terms of cash and currency. With your diplomatic engineering, you know how to turn on the power and keep things moving. You can dodge any question that does not have prosperity written over it. An excellent organizer or buyer, your keen memory for names and faces is an asset—yet sometimes it pays to forget. If you have a grudge to shed, prepare to shed it now. Don't worry about any water that has gone over the mill— you can build a greater fortune still. Love what you do, and those around you too, and you'll soon be moving on to larger freedom.

9 All the world loves a lover, and you could love the entire world. Sometimes, with your strong emotional nature, you almost succeed in doing just that. You enjoy long trips in this, or any other country, the longer the better. Some Nines give everything away, and even when they have little to give, that does not stop them from offering to share. Don't overdo it. You may be able to heal just by the laying on of hands.

10 See Number 1.

11 Born for the limelight, you are an able soul and have the makings of a master when you bridle your impulsive temperament and hold yourself in check until you find just the right atmosphere in which

[90]

to let your talents shine. Born for **adventure, go** slowly—"sharp curve ahead." A high-speed artist, sensitive and psychic, you may be away ahead of the other fellow. If you get fidgety, go to a movie, ride horseback, or just walk. Music should be an avenue of expression and interest, splendid for the nerves.

12 You are unusual in that you seem to fit in anywhere, yet there may be times when you wish to be alone just when company is coming. When you are home you wish to go somewhere, and when you are out you want to go home; yet you are very pleasant about it—let you alone, or pay no attention, and you will soon snap out of it and be the life of the party. All you need when you are out of sorts is something new to wear, nice and bright. You have so much within yourself, others are not really necessary, and yet you wish some friend around you just the same. Artistic, inventive, with a sense of humor, your life should be a full one.

13 You have a keen mind which is ever active. You should not tire easily, but in the event you feel a bit sarcastic, get something to eat that is sweet, then turn on the radio for some music, or sketch some cartoons for your own amusement. In that state your smile will absorb all the trouble around, and all will be romantic—for the moment. You are too busy to dwell with romance long. Your humor may be a bit late at times, but you can make others laugh with deliberate design. Mathematics may prove of value to you and aid you in furthering your pet scheme. Don't be too severe with yourself or others. Plan to Play.

14 You need a varied outlet for your emotional nature —you are very sensitive, so is the rest of the family. You are easygoing so long as the going is easy, then you may become evasive or yield to temper because of your impatience. You always know how to improve another's plan, so do the same with your own when you discover the need. Your judgment is good, occasionally. Be careful of extremes. Your hat hangs on a peg by the door ready to go when you let your duty complex rest a bit. Your right hand may not know what your left hand is doing, but that's all right, just so you allow the other person a like amount of freedom.

15 Affectionate, generous, interested in the welfare of others, don't deprive them of their lesson or experience by doing for them what they should do for themselves. With an urge to go, yet a sense of responsibility in your present duties, you may have a difficult time deciding which path to take. Seek out a 7 who really knows for a little private counsel, and you may emerge with a real plan. You are a good talker, but make it snappy, don't argue. Your ability to investigate and improve educational, hygienic, or athletic standards might make you a professional counselor in such fields. You love a home, but take a frequent trip away now and then and you will love it better.

16 You are refined, almost extravagant in your good taste; industrious, almost religious in the performance of your duties, as everything you do must be *the last word*. You are serious, yet have a droll humor; determined and wilful, yet sensitive, with feelings easily hurt, until you learn to close your aura and throw off any outer atmosphere. Deaf to suggestions, even when they are right, yet able to triumph over obstacles, you may have to be pushed onto the stage. But once there, you will surprise your audience with knowledge they never dreamed you possessed. Have confidence, let your intuition come through, and you will speak with authority.

17 You are an excellent judge of quality and could be a successful buyer of antiques. Any idea to receive your appraisal or comment should be presented complete—you have no time for discussion of half-formed plans. You know how to keep a secret and expect the same cooperation in others. You have a distinctive way about you and may appear to have more money than you really have, or you may have more than some of your friends suspect, hid under the hall stair carpet or in grandfather's clock, but more likely in government bonds. As a member of some exclusive golf or country club you should find those associates you deem worthwhile.

18 You are an artist in a big way, perhaps of big business—the larger your swing around the world, the better. You know how to balance intellect with understanding, and bring practical service and sympathy to friends or associates. Prosperous-looking, you should not complain if you are called upon to give and give. If others use you, blame no one but yourself. Have no fears for your own affairs, they will come out O. K., if you find an excuse for an occasional business trip and get a larger and broader view. Some Nines make a business of love and some love their business better--you are the balanced type who should set an example for the rest of us.

19 You can finish one thing and without waiting for an inspiration (which seems perennial with you) have something new and different to offer immediately. A dual nature, you can be a clinging vine, or utterly detached. Learn to love yourself, as you are your own best and closest friend. You can adjust yourself to the entire world with an understanding that is quite incomprehensible to the lower Numbers. Creative, artistic, you can see beauty in all things, but don't spend so much time furnishing ideas to others that you fail to arrive yourself. You are the Sun in your world—keep on shining.

20 A born analyst, you are able to attract wealth and travel the world o'er when you learn to analyze diplomatically and join your idea with another idea, or person, so that both are happy and harmonious. Music should appeal to you, and imitative ability should be a part of your endowment. Cooperation, patience and diplomacy are your keys for winning others over to your way of thinking. You are vain about your feet, so do not pay more for your shoes than you should, but give one foot a little more exercise by putting it and your talents forward. We advise gold, rather than a platinum ring for you.

21 You have that ever youthful spirit that should grow younger each year after you are 45. The high standard of perfection you demand of yourself and your friend may make it difficult for both, yet your genial good nature, even though it be tinged with satire now and then, makes you distinctly worth having on one's social list. An excellent entertainer, distinctive in your style, you bring us that breath of spring which makes us want to start and live over again. Watch the diet, go slow with the sweets. Swing high, swing low; swing to, swing fro, but don't try to do it all at once. Choose your own middle ground.

22 Lord of all you survey, commanding attention in your every mood, yet intuitive enough to catch the mood of another on the wing, you are one to be reckoned with in this day of political intrigue, for when you set your sails to catch the wind which wafts the trend of favors, there is apt to be a movement outward, by others, by reason of schemes which you uncover. More successful in a foreign clime than in your native land, able to handle groups diplomatically, a gambler in spirit with the big things you deem worthwhile, yet a lucky one at that, you can scarcely be classed with the rest of us. Your world is of your own making, so you can take it as that—a master builder who can swing from earth to heaven and back again, and make us think we can do it too. Are we glad we met you? Yes!

23* You can be an excellent character analyst, just as a social diversion, or sell your service too as an entertainer. You can point out defects with a sense of humor and make us laugh at our own idiosyncrasies too. Growing younger and younger as time passes is a pastime with you. Two friends of the opposite sex you should be able to handle at the same time and still keep friendly with both. Unusual—clever, here today and gone tomorrow, but we're mighty glad you came.

* If your name has more than 23 letters, reduce the number. For example, for 24 letters read Number 6; for 25, Number 7 etc.

Chapter IV

MISSING NOTES

No one can appreciate anything outside of his own vibration. It is no more possible for another to see your point of view at all times than it is for a man in a high-powered car to bring back the same report of territory covered as that of an aviator flying above him. The stories would be entirely different, yet each would be right, according to the point of view.

Anyone who is minus certain numbers in his name is either weak or lacking in the qualities which such numbers represent, and one should not expect the impossible. This does not mean that they should not be developed, but it does give greater tolerance in the present situation.

Having set out your full birth name, if any one of the nine numbers be lacking, look for the counteracting influence below. Incorporate this quality into your consciousness and you will have completed your octave, on which a perfect symphony may now be played, for you will understand the one type of person who before seemed *impossible*. You will have a new love.

Lacking 1. Build up more faith in yourself and your plan. Have more *nerve,* decide for yourself, and act accordingly. Do something *different,* that will make you stand out above the average.

Lacking 2. Develop more system, coordination, and sense of time. Make a schedule for each day the night before, then follow it through. Listen to what the other person has to say. Analyze it but withhold your opinion until later, when you can give a good-natured remedy or reply. Associate more with groups, and work with another happily. Let your jewelry be gold.

Lacking 3. Develop your bump of humor. Make a collection of first-class stories and then entertain your friends with a bit of humor on every social occasion. This will make you still more popular. Find the color that is most becoming and dress in the lighter shades. Learn to dance, take some lessons in writing or sketching, get acquainted with the children. Develop your creative ability in that line which you enjoy most.

Lacking 4. Don't be afraid to soil your hands. They will stand all the wear that you may give them. A hobby in the arts and crafts which especially appeals to you would help your sense of proportion and line. Keep track of income and expenses, and check up on yourself with a diary of events.

Whether musical or not, learn to sing, play, or hum some march-time music. This will help to establish the 4-rhythm in your nature which is lacking. This in turn will supply your missing note and establish balance and harmony twixt your mind and emotions.

Lacking 5. Don't be afraid of the opposite sex. They have some lessons for you. Daily association with various types of mind will make your own more agile. If compelled to deal with the public or present an idea to others, don't decline. No matter how difficult it may be, it will make a new person of you in a short time. Travel as much as you can, the more the better, and don't be afraid to make a frequent change in location. Walk, dance, be athletic. Wear a different costume each day, change the furniture around, and we'll even allow you to change your mind. Your last plan may be better.

Lacking 6. A home of your own will give you a more established background. Attract it, if you have it not. Be a genial host. Develop your voice. Take some speaking lessons which will give you all the confidence in the world in expressing your views before others. Responsibility, graciously assumed, may open a door to greater happiness than you dream. Socially or professionally, lend the benefit of your counsel to those less fortunate than yourself.

Lacking 7. Learn to finish what you start. Give yourself an incentive to reach a certain goal by a given time. Spend your weekends in the country and arrange a quiet time for yourself each day. Be an authority on *something*, even if it be only your own pet hobby. Set an example of dignity, culture, and perfect grocming to your friends. Keep your own counsel and the confidence of others. *Relax.* Get acquainted with nature. Play golf, do anything which recharges your physical magnetism through contact with Mother Earth. Study philosophy, and get a new slant on life.

Lacking 8. Financial problems may be your difficulty. Learn to get value received, whether you are buying materials, talent, or service. Organize your time so that it counts for the most to you. Associate with and observe those who have touched the key to material wealth, which 8 the $ represents. You should become rich in this world's goods if you add this missing note to your scale. Tact and diplomacy will hasten the day.

Lacking 9. Radiate love and good will toward everyone, no matter how painful the giving may be. Criticize not. Everyone is running true to form according to his nature. Knowing why people do as they do, and that each one has his own lesson to learn, relieves you of any responsibility of passing judgment.

The more of the world you see, and the farther you go, the broader your view and the more you know, the greater will be your sympathy for those less fortunate than yourself. Whoever knows the most must needs make the adjustment, therefore it is up to you to be the big, magnanimous soul who overlooks the shortcomings of others because of your greater understanding. You know that if one desires love, he first sets it in motion where he is, and by so doing, the world and all there is in it becomes his.

Chapter V

HOW TO REACH YOUR HEART

If you would win the favor of others, or if they would win yours, observe the *first vowel* of the name most fre quently used. The vowels are A-E-I-O-U and sometimes Y, and W when combined with another vowel, to make a diphthong. For the rules governing vowels see any collegiate or unabridged dictionary.

Your first vowel, especially of your original name, shows your instinctive reaction to outer stimuli. It registers your emotional impulse, being more dynamic when standing as the first letter of the name than when preceded by a consonant. An "A" vowel would be interested in a new idea, but if the "A" were preceded by "D", "M", or "V", the individual would be more conservative, he would want to know, "How' much will it cost? Will it work? Is it practical?"

IF YOUR FIRST VOWEL IS "A"

You are responsive to new ideas, but prefer that they come from your own fertile brain than from that of another. You are not in the least impressed by what Mr., Miss, or Mrs. "So-and-So" has or does. It matters not if the whole world decrees that such and such a thing be proper, you enjoy being different. Old reliable methods arouse only antagonism in you. But give you an element of chance, something to do that has never been done before, and you will be all attention.

You do not stop to look around, nor care whether others accompany you—the *first at the top* generally arrives alone. Alone, but not lonesome, for in your own inimitable self you have a host of good company.

IF YOUR FIRST VOWEL IS "E"

You love variety,—and have that magnetism which makes for popularity with the opposite sex. Intriguing, versatile and adaptable, you must have freedom, action, and a frequent change. An excellent judge of character, you know how to ward off the inquiring remarks of another, although you may be able to unearth his whole life history. Able to present your idea in an interesting or entertaining way, you convey the impression that one is really missing a thrilling adventure if he does not accept your proposal, whatever it be. We hope you have been clever enough to find that niche which relieves you of too much regularity, or conformity, for you are the spice of life to the rest of us, though an eternal enigma to the Even Numbers. Able to look both ways, at apparently the same time, you are an incentive to agility—but don't break too many hearts.

IF YOUR FIRST VOWEL IS "I"

You are interested in the *big idea*, in travel, or the artistic, humanitarian side of life. You want the whole world, and scarcely less will satisfy you. Sympathetic and emotional, often too much so for your own good, you have that radiant love quality which carries a healing atmosphere to those whom you seek to revivify. Generous, often beyond the point of justice to yourself, do not be concerned if others fail to return an equal measure of thoughtfulness or service to you. Learn to deal justly with yourself and leave the rest with the Universal Mind. Criticize not—it will spoil your beauty. With your strong magnetism, whatever you send out returns in like abundant measure. Resent not—ever! Love even the worst of us, and we will send you back a love thought to blossom later as a rose.

IF YOUR FIRST VOWEL IS "O"

Responsibility helps you to raise your self-esteem. The more chance you have to advise or counsel others, the more useful you are, hence as a professional consultant, or teacher, or mother, you have a chance to radiate your

[99]

true light. Cultivate your speaking or singing voice. Take an interest in community affairs. Be a convincing speaker, but do not argue. Match intellectual swords, but see that you carry your point tactfully, by the pure logic of your reasoning and your compelling knowledge, of the true state of affairs. A genial host, we hope you'll invite us to tea some day.

IF YOUR FIRST VOWEL IS "U"

You are a jolly sort, and we like you. We only wish we could excel you in your colorful repartee. As an after dinner speaker, a genial friend, or one who can write a truly personal letter, you provide that spark which almost makes us a self-starter too. A good judge of perfumes, a lover of flowers and plants, able to make them bloom when others fail, you are the distiller of those essences in life which makes us love that fleeting beauty which may come and go, yet lifts us up to a greater understanding. Yours is the colorful life, adding color to our own. We'll don our best when calling on you.

IF YOUR VOWEL IS "Y"

You have a strong Intuition and should heed it. While you may love to keep some things to yourself, and not let even your best friend know, while you always appear to have something *up your sleeve*, still you are worth cultivating, for the opportunity it gives to unmask scientifically the most difficult type of human nature to understand. And, as might be expected, when we do learn to gain your hearty response, it is far more than anticipated.

You do not cast your pearls before the uncouth. One must register a certain amount of perfection or depth of understanding to bring out the deep things you know. They are worth all the effort one can put forth, and more—if he doesn't believe it, he should try. Your love for penetrating the deeper whys and wherefores gains for you an authoritative knowledge. Your opinion upon weighty matters should be asked, and then an exit made, not waiting for a reply. If it be worth your while, you will be responding with your own added suggestion by and by.

IF FIRST VOWELS BE "OY" AS IN ROY

You combine the qualities of 6 and 7 which make 13 or 4. You know how to take a discussion and an authoritative opinion, and boil them both down into concrete facts. Then if they stand the test of your measuring rule, one can depend upon it, they are worth while. Unless one can support his argument with proof as to how, why, and the cost and time entailed, he had better not ask for an hour of your valuable time. But if he know, and knows that he knows and can present a logical reason therefor, let him radiate all the power he has, in a diplomatic way, and he will find a foundation, as well as a support for his plan.

IF YOUR FIRST VOWELS BE "EW" AS IN LEWIS

The diphthong here is composed of two 5's, making a 10 or 1. You have the qualities of the "A" vowel to a certain extent, which you may investigate, but in addition, the opposite sex is far more important to you than it is to them. In fact, without working with them or through them, it would be difficult to accomplish the larger things. If you suffer because of them, it is just to teach you some vital lesson, for when you know how to handle, through intuitive understanding, each person who crosses your path, your door to success will swing wide open. You should be able to sell or present to the public almost any idea of merit dealing with the principle of rejuvenation in a new and vital way, and that in turn is what would have a special appeal for you.

IF YOUR FIRST VOWELS BE "OW" AS IN BROWN

The diphthong of 6 and 5 makes 11, the inspirational quality which enables you to be a real light in your world and to help others see farther. You need the opposite sex to counsel with, and if you'll have a little patience with his shortcomings until you lead him up gradually, from where he is, to your point of view, life should be much happier for both of you. Don't let others rule you, because if you do, your 11 becomes a 2, and then undecided as to what you should do, you lose your own inner center

[101]

of poise and are compelled to shine only by the reflected light of a stronger mind. You belong in the limelight where, seeing your beam, others may take new courage from the stimulating, dynamic, penetrating, and almost hypnotic power which has been accorded you. Use it wisely.

Chapter VI

CHARACTER SKETCHING WITH CHARACTER GRAMS

Gram is "a suffix indicating drawing, writing."— Webster.

Drawing a word picture of your colorful traits may be made a pleasurable pastime and reveal an artist in your midst.

The most complete character view that could be accorded you, would be, of course, a composite of your varied traits as they appear to your friends and associates. Such a vivid light upon your manifold nature may be easily had by allowing each one in your present circle to set down his opinion in writing.

Toward this end provide each player with pencil and paper the moment he is seated, before the Guardian begins to read the Name and reveal the Secrets, as outlined in Part II, Chapter II. As the Guardian proceeds, each player fills in for future use, the proper Number in each of the following spaces. (If you have the list ready, typed or written, so much the better.)

Full Name total.............................

Last Name total.............................

First Name total.............................

Number of Letters in Name...................

Numbers Lacking......................... ...

Present Name total.........................

Birth Date total.............................

After Guardian discloses the varied slants on your good nature, ten minutes may be allowed for those sitting in council to write a brief word portrait of the one whose name has been read, using as a guide, the Numbers on their list. With these at their command they may search through Character Traits and other useful words in Part II, Chapters X and XI, or build words of their own. For a brief sketch of Edison and John Barrymore, see Part I, Chapter X.

A prize may be given for the most *Characteristic* sketch.

Chapter VII

YOUR WHEEL OF FORTUNE

CYCLES

"To everything there is a season, and
A Time to every purpose under the heaven."

All constructive growth proceeds logically, each succeeding step including all that have gone before, plus one more. This law of numerical progression from zero (0) to 9 is reflected in Nature and in man's activities as the unfoldment of both. It shows the path to realization in the shortest length of time.

The cipher (0) or *seed* in nature, is followed by *1*, the *generation of motion* or life,—*the planting season*. In the *2nd* stage we have generation below and cultivation above the soil, *two processes* going on *at the same time*. In *3*, *growth* above the ground, to the ripened grain. In *4*, grain ground into flour is made *usable and practical*. In *5*, the flour is *sold* to baker. Here it *changes hands and places*, in keeping with the changing aspect of *5*. In *6* the flour is put to *useful service* in food. In *7*—*Finish*, and *recognition of merit* comes through the distinctive manner in which the food is served,—and enjoyably eaten. In *8*, the digestive process acts as a *transformer*, turning the food into body *building* elements. In *9*, the *Circulation* of chemical properties from the food, throughout the body, complete the first cycle—and *keep things moving,*—reflecting the realization or essence of the previous 8 steps outwardly, in H E A L T H

8 5 1 3 2 8 = 2 7 = (9).

[105]

0=The Realm of Ideas.
1 Definite Idea or decision upon new plan.
2 Cultivation of plan by analysis and gathering materials.
3 Plan in visibility—the complete model.
4 Idea in usable, concrete form—a machine built, or book printed (after being written in 3).
5 Idea sold or presented to public, which may necessitate improvement or change.
6 Established Service. Personnel or public educated to the proper use or higher standard.
7 Recognition by reason of Quality, finish, technique.
8 Larger expansion and greater financial return. The perfection of original plan from 1 to 7 may bring demand for new units to be set in operation, in different places, or on a larger scale.
9 Realization, publicity, money, travel, letting go of the old, contacting other parts of the world for new Ideas to be set in motion in the following period of 10.

Harmony depends upon one's being in tune with the rhythm of energy about him, for in *rhythmic periods of time*, man lives and moves and has his being. Upon recognition and acceptance of a *timely period for change*, depends his early success or ultimate achievement. Solomon, the wisest of men, who is said to be the author of Ecclesiastes, portrays the picture so clearly, we are quoting him:

ECCLESIASTES: CHAPTER 3

Verse 1 "To everything there is a season, and a Time to every purpose under the heaven.
2 A Time to be born, and a time to die; a time to plant and a time to pluck up that which is planted;
3 A Time to heal; a time to break down, and a time to build up;
4 A Time to weep, and a time to laugh; a time to mourn, and a time to dance;

5   A Time to cast away stones, and a time to gather stones together; a time to embrace, and a time to refrain from embracing; (5 is the principle of discard, improvement, and association with the opposite sex.)

6   A Time to get, and a time to lose; a time to keep, and a time to cast away;

7   A Time to rend, and a time to sew; a time to keep *silence* (the attribute of 7), and a time to speak.

8   A Time to love, and a time to hate; a time of war, and a time of peace.

15 *That which hath been is now; and*
    That which is to be hath already been.

22 Wherefore, I perceive that *there is nothing better than that a man should rejoice in his own works; for that is his portion.*"

The Octave represents one cycle of expression, in its 7 notes, and one more, making 8, to complete the scale. The 8th note is said to have twice the number of vibrations per second as the 1st. 9 represents the principle of the Whole—the cohesive, motivating force which links one with another and blends them into one complete cycle of harmony.

7 marks the peak of individual effort, and of the average cycle. 8 signifies its crystallized form.

9, the disappearing number (add 9 to any number and reduce the total, and the primary value remains the same)—is the swirl or the swing, which takes the whole world which you have created in the eight preceding steps and moves it forward into the next cycle.

In the realm of the emotions 9 is the Love number which makes the world go round in your locality and keeps things running smoothly. In the mental world 9 represents thought, which makes one's ideas go round—to the point of decision and action,—if you keep your thoughts in control—otherwise you may be "going round in circles" unable to figure a way out. The way out comes in 1—a Decision.

[107]

TIMELY PERIODS FOR CHANGE

Every year in a cycle has its particular purpose. When the direction of energy begins to turn, as it must do after every 4th step, one must be willing to let go,—and move with the current. If in 5 or 9, one insists upon holding on to the old, he will find himself left behind, going round the same old cycle of activities again.

Growth comes through change,—change in the right direction at the right time.

The following chapter will suggest briefly the changes which may be in store for you in the present or near future.

Chapter VIII

THIS YEAR'S ADVENTURE FOR YOU

Find age on last birthday in table below. First group of numbers adds to 10, second to 2 or 11, third to 3, etc. showing whether you are in 1st, 2nd, 3rd, 4th or later period of present cycle.

The time from birth to end of first year represents the 0 or realm of possibilities from whence all else proceeds. Not until the child has lived one full year do we say he is One year old. The full influence of any year cannot be felt until we have lived through that year, hence the numbers given here register your present age on any legal record.

1st Year in New Cycle

1—10—19—28—37—46—55 — 64 — 73 — 82 — 91 —100.

2nd Year

2—11—20—29—38—47—56 — 65 — 74 — 83 — 92 —101.

3rd Year

3—12—21—30—39—48—57 — 66 — 75 — 84 — 93 —102.

4th Year

4—13—22—31— 40 – 49 –58 — 67 — 76 — 85 — 94 —103.

5th Year

5—14—23—32—41—50—59 — 68 — 77 — 86 — 95 —104.

6th Year

6—15—24—33—42—51—60 — 69 — 78 — 87 — 96
—105.

7th Year

7—16—25—34—43—52—61 — 70 — 79 — 88 — 97
—106.

8th Year

8—17—26—35—44—53—62 — 71 — 80 — 89 — 98
—107.

9th Year

9—18—27—36—45—54—63 — 72 — 81 — 90 — 99
—108.

THIS YEAR FOR YOU

1st Year in New Cycle

1—10—19—28—37—46—55—64—73—82—91—100

This is a decision year. Be receptive to a new idea.
Decide for yourself! DO something *different.* Be original, surprise your friends. Start "the ball rolling" to
bring your own personal ambition into expression. Make
the most of your social contacts.

BUT—*Keep your plans to yourself.* Tell no one until
they are carefully grown and completed. New Ideas are
very "sensitive" to cold draughts, or critical opinion,
or well-meant suggestions from friends, family or associates. They have to be reared carefully by one's own
hand.

Be willing to let go of the old to make room for
the new. *Listen to your Intuition,* act upon it. Put your
best foot forward, with a *fearless* spirit, and the next
twelve months should open new doors of opportunity
and growth for you.

2nd Year in Cycle

2—11—20—29—38—47—56—65—74—83—92—101

This is a year to make the most of your social contacts. Enjoy life. New friends among the opposite sex

[110]

may bring added thrill or adventure. **Make an effort
to contact important people.** Put your best foot forward, let your light shine. A favorable period for *selling* well organized, entertaining, or artistic, *creative
effort.* A new interest in children, or expressing your
talent in some new way should make for variety and
growth. Travel if you can. Make each day more colorful than the last.

3rd Year of Cycle
3—12—21*—30—39—48—57—66—75—84—93—102

This is a year to put health and affairs in perfect
order. Give yourself a once-over from a physical standpoint—or have your health adviser do so. Bring greater
regularity into your program; allow a definite time for
relaxation in the out of doors. This year should mark
your real start toward the development of previous
hopes and plans. Combine social activities with a definite
purpose; save yourself the friction of inharmonious associations. Study the theatre; occupy the stage in your
world. Become an authority on *something,* even if it be
only your pet hobby.

4th Year of Cycle
4—13—22†—31—40—49—58—67—76—85—94—103

This year is favorable for a change of location or improvement in your daily schedule. Take a trip if you
can; investigate new fields or figure out how to handle
your present one in a more efficient way. Consider the
opposite sex in your plans, they may be able to help you.

* If you are 21, you are in your 22nd year. Finish to perfection your education or present duties. Do not tie yourself up
with matrimonial contracts or gold-brick schemes. After you
are twenty-four, you will be a better judge,—not only of personalities, but of propositions. Next year you should take the
longest trip possible.

† If you are 22, it is important to broaden your view. Take
the longest trip you can,—on the water if possible. Put forth
your best effort, diplomatically, to meet important people, or
those of large affairs. Polish your talents until they shine.

[111]

5th Year of Cycle
5—14—23—32—41—50—59—68—77—86—95—104

This should give you an inspirational new beginning by reason of a change of residence or trip away from home. Add to your knowledge in some way. Bring variety into your program. Investigate. Listen to your intuition and act upon it. Be clever in your association with the opposite sex. Meet their WHYs with your WHEREFOREs. Find his or her center of interest,—stimulate that if you wish a favorable response to your own suggestion.

6th Year of Cycle
6—15—24—33—42—51—60—69—78—87—96—105

Favorable for the establishment of a home or a more definite professional or business background. Keep busy, master all details, make your duties shine with the polish of perfection. Figure out some way to save time or do the same thing with less effort. Build your idea into definite form—this is a year to lay the corner stone—and complete the foundation of your real air castle.

7th Year of Cycle
7—16—25—34—43—52—61—70—79—88—97—106

This year indicates a finishing or completion of certain business affairs affecting the home or profession. Your success lies in being a diplomat, knowing when to speak and when to keep silence. Uncover the motive of the other person before you express your views. If called upon to speak before any groups or organizations, by all means do so. Be the gracious host to professional associates. Responsibility efficiently carried through should bring excellent return to you next year.

8th Year of Cycle
8—17—26—35—44—53—62—71—80—89—98—107

This year should bring a larger financial return, dependent upon the well organized and completed effort of the seven preceding years. Turn over any lesser details to others and work out a larger and more ambitious program. Favorable for buying, investments, business contracts. Associate with those groups or organizations which can boost you along in the direction you desire to go. Be a master diplomat, yet exercise a fighting spirit if need be in order that justice, equity and the proper compensation may prevail, on all occasions.

9th Year of Cycle

9—18—27—36—45—54—63—72—81—90—99—108

This year marks the ending of a cycle, when you must be willing to let go of old associations or attachments, if need be, in order that you may be free to move on into a new environment or fresh activity next year. If you refuse to move on at this time—and literally, you should take a trip if you possibly can—you are apt to be swept into the reverse current and have to repeat a similar round of experiences again. Have the nerve to take a chance with a new idea if you would benefit by the new door of opportunity which awaits you the coming year. If impossible to travel—at least go in your imagination—*Love Yourself*. Duty begins with *Yourself* this year,—if you would blossom and bloom for the next nine years. Make your Decisions when alone—keep them well guarded,—and you may surprise your friends in the near future.

Chapter IX

CHARACTER GRAMS "BAEDECKER"

WHERE DO WE GO FROM HERE?—LIST OF STATES AND
CITIES—FOREIGN COUNTRIES

ın what state or country were you born?

The atmosphere of that locality, surcharged with the thought of that day, inbreathed with your first breath, left an indelible impress upon your sensitive nature. Herein lies one of the hidden secrets of your later subconscious reaction to outer stimuli.

A study of nationalities will give you some concept of the principle. Both Germany and France total 11. Both of them will occupy the limelight (11) in this world's affairs, so long as they continue to exist—and should they disappear they would go out with a blaze of glory, or a conflagration. Their light cannot be hid.

Germany with a 4 vowel and 7 consonant, stands as the last word in scientific (7) mechanical (4) achievement, while the march time beat of 4—the inner consciousness, registers outwardly in the martial strains of the soldiers, in their regular and thorough military training.

France, on the other hand, with a 6 vowel and 5 consonant, shows a greater freedom between the sexes (5), and a greater interest in beauty and clothes—the 6 principle. As the style center of the world, France may continue to hold her own despite the efforts of the U. S. A. to wield the sceptre from her.

In the States, people born in Illinois (9) have a love for travel and usually do see a good share of the world. If they do not go in person, they bring the world to them—Chicago with its two World Fairs, and as a meeting place for the World Fellowship of Faiths expresses the universal spirit which the 9 vibration of the State typifies.

New York with its total of 3, is the home of the writer (3) and entertainer (3)—being a center for the stage and for the publishing field in the U. S. A.

California with its total of 7 reflects the Nature (7) aspect, in the beauty of the great out-doors, in the mountains, with the secrets (a 7 principle) which they hold, and the heights to which they go.

Ohio, which totals 11 has produced more Presidents ("President" is 11) than any other state in the Union with the exception of Virginia. Eight have come from Virginia, seven from Ohio. *But*—seven out of eight from Virginia were born *before 1800*. Since Ohio actually came into the limelight as a State,—1803, it has given birth to Seven Presidents, Virginia, One.

If you are contemplating a change of any kind, observe the rhythm of the state in which you were born—then look for the same rhythm elsewhere, and you should feel at home.

The Vowel of any country, city or state, shows what the people of that locality *desire*. Therefore observe also the vowels. If the Total of your name, last name, or full signature is the same as the Vowel of any city or country—you *are* the type of person, or *can do*, the things which they desire. You should be able to supply their demand, and in return they should compensate you.

U. S. A.

STATES	Total No.	IMPORTANT CITIES	Total No.	Vowels
Alabama	4	Akron	5	7
Arkansas	3	Atlanta	6	3
Arizona	3	Atlantic City	11	11-7
California	7	Baltimore	5	3
Colorado	11	Birmingham	4	10
Connecticut	10	Boston	22	3
Delaware	6	Buffalo	9	10
District of Columbia	10	Chicago	10	7
Florida	11	Cincinnati	6	10
Georgia	8	Cleveland	6	11
Idaho	10	Columbus	7	3
Illinois	9	Denver	5	10
Indiana	7	Des Moines	4	7
Iowa	3	Detroit	10	2
Kansas	11	Fort Worth	8	3
Kentucky	11	Grand Rapids	3	11
Louisiana	11	Hollywood	3	7
Maine	6	Indianapolis	6	8
Maryland	7	Kansas City	11-3	9
Massachusetts	6	Los Angeles	10	8
Michigan	10	Louisville	10	5
Minnesota	11	Miami	9	10
Mississippi	4	Milwaukee	10	5
Missouri	6	Minneapolis	10	3
Montana	6	New Haven	11	11
Nebraska	8	New Orleans	9	8
Nevada	2	New York	3	7
New Hampshire	4	Oakland	22	8
New Jersey	7	Omaha	2	8
New Mexico	3	Philadelphia	11	7
New York	3	Pittsburgh	5	3
North Carolina	4	Portland	10	7
North Dakota	10	Providence	3	7
Ohio	11	Reno	7	11
Oklahoma	4	Rochester	3	7
Oregon	11	Salt Lake City	11-10	5
Pennsylvania	8	San Antonio	5	5
Rhode Island	10	San Francisco	5	8
South Carolina	3	Scranton	5	7
South Dakota	9	Seattle	10	11
Tennessee	7	Springfield	11	5
Texas	6	St. Louis	3-22	9
Utah	5	St. Paul	8	4
Vermont	8	Syracuse	3	7
Virginia	8	Tampa	6	2
Washington	4	Toledo	8	8
West Virginia	3	Trenton	7	11
Wisconsin	8	Tulsa	10	4
Wyoming	7	Washington	4	7

COUNTRIES

	Total No.	Vowel	
Africa	11	11	(a hidden 22)
Belgium	6	8	
Canada	6	3	
China	8	10	
Denmark	3	6	
England	3	6	
France	11	6	
Germany	11	4	
Greece	7	6	
Holland	3	7	
India	10	10	(a hidden 20)
Italy	22	8	"occult"
Japan	6	2	
Russia	6	4	
Spain	5	10	
Sweden	7	10	

Chapter X

CHARACTER TRAITS—VOCATIONS—PASTIMES

ACCORDING TO NUMBER VALUE OF WORD

Each word adds up to the Number under which it is shown.

A Pastime may become an Avocation—and eventually a Vocation.

NUMBER 1

	Traits		Activities
Positive	*Reverse or Negative*	*Vocation*	*Pastime or Avocation*
Ambitious	Timid	Air activities	Accordion
Aristocratic	Retiring	Artisan	Barber
Bachelor	Hermit	Aviation	Caddy
Dare	Evade	Emissary	Children
Foresee	Regret	Geographer	Circus
Hero	Coward	Guide	Geologist
Initiative	Lazy	Pioneer	Races
Win	Fail	Writing	Swim

NUMBER 2

Alert	Elude	Agent	Diet
Analyst	Crank	Analyst	Dress
Attract	Covet	Beauty	Drum
Beauty	Decay	Gold mining	Farm
Kind	Cross	Judge	Music
Steady	Flit	Music	Occult
On Time	Later	Shoe business	Seer
Wise	Dunce	Watch-making	Show

NUMBER 3

Traits			Activities
Positiv.	Reverse or Negative	Vocation	Pastime or Avocation
Absorbed	Idler	Actor	Band
Brave	Afraid	Army	Hunting
Friendly	Critical	Doctor	Bookstore
Good Nature	Sarcastic	Entertainer	Charity
Happy	Hysterical	Lawyer	Clubman
Humanitarian	Egotistical	Nursing	Pictures
Observing	Drift	Promoter	Poster making
Romantic	Radical	Writer	Wood carving

NUMBER 4

Adroit	Blunder	Accountant	Dominoes
Booster	Caustic	Apothecary	Alchemy
Brief	Gushing	Banking	Drawing.
Communicative	Gossip	Biology	Fencing
Confidential	Babbling	Collector	Fiddler
Conscientious	Deceitful	Design	Gymnastics
Ethical	Fanatical	Fiction	Politics
Fearless	Impetuous	Playwright	Reading

NUMBER 5

Awake	Drowsy	Arbitrator	Alderman
Brisk	Impatience	Automobile	Astronomy
Captivating	Egotist	Aviator	Ball Player
Explorer	Foolhardy	Conductor	Theatre
Frank	Sensitive	Craftsman	Boating
Intuition	Impulse	Engineer	Stunts
Power	Temper	Explorer	Camera
Willing	Defiant	Life Insurance	Vaudeville

NUMBER 6

Ability	Aimless	Adviser	Accompanist
Absorbing	Boastful	Architect	Collaborator
Active	Cramped	Bishop	Dramatic affairs
Compassionate	Crude	Bookseller	Educator
Decision	Hesitant	Dean—Teacher	Musical affairs
Benevolent	Selfish	Hotel field	Psychologist
Knowledge	Visionary	Justice	Discussion
Appeal	Bashful	Textiles	Costumer

NUMBER 7

Positive	Traits Reverse or Negative	Vocation	Activities Pastime or Avocation
Authoritative	Curious	Assessor	Antiques
Courage	Egotism	Farmer	Athletics
Dignity	Aloofness	Financier	Racing
Idealist	Complainer	Finisher	Church
Now	Last	Psycho-analyst	Puzzle
Polished	Crusty	Real estate	Investments
Specific	Secretive	Stage	Sculptor
Wit	Argue	Steel worker	Gardening

NUMBER 8

Analytical	Contradict	Accounting	Athlete
August	Acrid	Actuary	Musical Comedy
Anticipate	Almost	Builder	Climber
Buoyant	Impatient	Chain store	Books
Brain	Chasm	Delicatessen	Cook
Candid	Balk	Engineering	Sports
Cordial	Deceptive	Mail Service	Religion
Tact	Critic	Railway Service	Swimming

NUMBER 9

Aesthetic	Barbaric	Bonds	Agriculture
Artistic	Plodding	Cashier	Baseball
Breezy	Daze	Clothier	Croquet
Cool-headed	Combative	Decorator	Checkers
Congenial	Cynic	Designer	Cards
Conqueror	Cowardice	Law	Hand-ball
Dazzling	Vulgar	Newspaper man	Fishing
Inspiration	Brood	Publicity	Dog races

NUMBER 11

Able	Apathetic	Advertising	Adventure
Admirable	Adverse	Author	Comedy
Adventurer	Absconder	Bacteriologist	Diving
Agreeable	Angry	Bookshop	Biography
Authentic	Braggart	Capitalist	Horse Racing
Creative	Doubtful	Education	Movies
Independent	Indifferent	Preacher	Cowboy
Psychic	Drone	Sailor	Radio

NUMBER 22

Traits		Activities	
Positive	Reverse or Negative	Vocation	Pastime or Avocation
Alive	Aloof	Attache	Traveler
Aglow	Asleep	Chef	Clown
Beacon	Crash	Clerk	Talkie
Broad	Stoop	Crew manager	Water sports
Capable	Bore	Food service	Sing
Noted	Flop	Head master	Polo
Speed	Fret	Master mechanic	Basket ball
Work (brain)	Storm (brain)	Statesman	Golf

Chapter XI

MUSIC, COLORS, FOODS, GEMS, FLOWERS

The rythm of greatest value to You, is that of your *Birthdate*—your normal energy urge. All things in life in rhythm with basic notes of your Birthdate,—Sign, Month, Day, Year and final Total, have some special meaning for you.

MUSIC in the key of your natal Sign, shown on page 56, may have an especial appeal. Many Aquarians (11th Sign) like especially the key of Bb—11th note of the octave. Strike the Key of your natal Sign, HUM on this tone. With this as the major note of your life song, build a chord up or down and Hummmmmm your own melody. Humming helps to harmonize the Inner and Outer nature and makes one more at peace with himself.

COLORS with same vibration as the *Vowels* of your Name may be in favor, but those in rhythm with your *Birthdate* Total, then with Month, Day and Year, should be healthfully stimulating. The same holds true of Foods, Gems and Flowers. Flower arrangements, including one from each note of your birthdate, would make an ideal Color combination for you.

Color-tones from each note in Birthdate may also be used in your living room. Tones in harmony with *Sign* and *Month* benefit the *Physical* or Health vibration,—those in harmony with your *Day*, stimulate the *Mind*. Color-tones in rhythm with the *Year* are good for the *Emotions*. Those with same note as *full Birthdate* should strengthen the *Spirit* and bid you rise to your own true place in the Sun, where all the Colors of the Rainbow are Yours to Command!

"Music lifts the Spirit, Color feeds the Soul."

Each word adds up to the Number under which it appears.

10—Accordion
Air
Chant
Clarinet
Contralto
Fast
Flute
Harpist
Jews'-harp
Measure
Medley
Piano
Piccolo
Opera
Organ
Song
Staccato

20—Aria
Bugle
Cello
Cymbal
Drum
Music
Pipe-organ

3—Band
Baritone
Chord
Chorus
Cornet
Ensemble
Pastoral
Trombone
Violinist

4—Composition
Fiddle
Fiddler
Guitar
Harmony

Instrumental
Lute
Organist
Scale

5—Bass
Bells
Composer
Melodious
Player
Rhythmic
Trumpet
Viola

6—Accompanist
Banjo
Concert
Cornetist
Dramatic
Hymn
Legato
Lyre
Mouth organ
Musical
Slow
Soft
Tune

7—Anthem
Ballet
Bandmaster (3-22)
Brilliant
Church
Classical
Dirge
Harp
Loud
Overture
Program
Solo
Staff

[123]

8—Cadence
Cellist
Choir
Clef
Climax
Musician
Orchestra
Revue
Serenade
Soprano
Trill
Ukulele
Violoncello

9—Band concert
Choral society
Expression
Grand Opera
Instrument
Play
Rhythmical
Strain

Symphony
Tenor
Tone
Violin
Voice

11—Baby-Grand
Drummer
Glee-Club (2-11)
Melody
Musicale
Piece
Radio
Rhythm

22—Bassoon
Carol
Lullaby
Reel
Sing
Touch

COLORS

1—Apricot
Beige
Crimson
Flame
Lilac
Turquoise
Rainbow Red

2—Gold
Salmon
Rainbow Orange

3—Amber
American Beauty
Orchid
Rainbow Yellow
Rose

4—Blue
Emerald
Green
Indigo
Rainbow Green

5—Auburn
Cherry
Corn
Lemon

Pink
Wisteria
Rainbow Blue

6—Gray
Heliotrope
Henna
Mulberry
Orange
Peach
Scarlet
Wine
Rainbow Indigo

7—Brick
Magenta
Poppy
Purple
Steel
Rainbow Violet

8—Bronze
Buff
Canary
Mauve
Plum
Tan

9—Apple Green
Brown
Lavender
Red
Sage Green
Taupe

11—Black
Jade

Sand
Violet
White
Yellow

22—Coral
Cream
Light Yellow

FOODS

Each word adds to Number under which it appears.

1—Apricot
Artichokes
Baked apple
Baked beans
Bluefish
Chocolate
Cocoa
Cress
Eggplant
Fillet
Halibut
Jelly
Lentils
Lobster
Meat loaf
Oats
Olives
Peanut butter
Pumpkin
Raisin pie
Roast beef
Salad
Tongue
Turkey
Walnut

2—Breast of lamb
Candy
Eggs
Fowl
Salmon
Walnuts

3—Beer
Bread
Cabbage
Cobbler

Doughnuts
Duck
Gooseberry
Grapes
Hominy
Lime jello
Liver
Meat
Peaches
Pickels
Pie
Potatoes
Prunes
Pudding
Romaine
Toast
Tomato
Whole wheat

4—Asparagus
Buckwheat
Butterscotch pie
Carrots
Chocolate pudding
Chop suey
Cod
Coffee
Chowder
Cranberries
Dates
Dried beef
Eel
Grapefruit
Grouse
Ham
Honey
Lima beans

Onion
Oysters
Parsnips
Pineapple
Pretzels
Pumpkin pie
Raspberries
Strawberries
Sweetbreads
Veal
Yams

5—Almond
Apple
Bass
Beet
Broccoli
Butter
Celery
Cherry
Cookies
Corn-beef
Cucumber
Custard
Endive
Figs
Greens
Lettuce
Marmalade
Melon
Mulberries
Onions
Pears
Raspberry
Strawberry
Tripe

6—Apples
Banana
Beets
Blackberries
Bran Muffins
Crab
Fish
Mushrooms
Mustard
Orange
Parsley
Peach
Pork
Potato

Quince
Rye bread
Sole
Spaghetti
Sweet potato

7—Bananas
Blackberry
Chops
Fritters
Goose
Herring
Horseradish
Omelet
Potato Chips
Rhubarb
Roast Pork
Scallops
Shredded Wheat
Smelts
Spinach
Steel cut oats
Vegetable

8—Apple Pie
Bacon
Baked Potatoes
Beef Tenderloin
Blueberries
Caramel
Cauliflower
Cereal
Chicken
Corn Bread
Cottage Cheese
Croquettes
Currant Jell
Custard Pie
Finnan Haddie
Frog Legs
Ice
Lemon Pie
Parfait
Raisins
Rice
Sardines
Soup
Tea
Veal Stew
Vegetables
Vegetable Salad
Waldorf Salad

9—Barley Broth
Beef
Cheese—Roquefort
Cheese Wafers
Coleslaw
Crabmeat
Jello
Junket
Milk
Orange Juice
Pastry
Plums
Pork Pie
Sauerkraut
Sweet Potato Pie
Syrup
Tomatoes
Turnips
Waffles
Watermelon

11—Apricots
Baked Potato
Bran Bread
Buns
Cake
Chestnut
Clam
Cocoanut

Gooseberries
Kale
Macaroni
Nuts
Plum Pudding
Radishes
Shrimp
Steak
String Beans
Sturgeon
Tapioca
Wild Rice

22—Cream
Cream Cheese (22-9)
Fig
Fruit Cake
Ice Cream (8-22)
Limes
Mutton
Oatmeal
Pear
Pecans
Prune Whip
Rolls
Smoked Tongue (22-10)
Sour Cream (10-22)
Squash
Water Cress (22-10)

GEMS AND STONES

Each word adds to Number under which it appears.

0—Lodestone
Aquamarine
Moss Agate
Turquoise

20—Gold

3—Amber
Amethyst
Ruby
Sardonyx

4—Blood stone
Emerald
Moonstone
Ochre
Silver

5—Brass
Nephrite

6—Diamond
Jasper
Marble
Onyx
Topaz

7—Alabaster
Agate
Carat
Pearl
Platinum

8—Beryl
Bronze
Chrysolite

[127]

Crystal
Mica
Opal
Pearls
Scarab

9—Nickel
Opals

11—Garnet
Jacinth
Jade
Sapphire

22—Coral

FLOWERS AND TREES

Each word adds up to Number under which it appears.

10—Azalea
Clematis
Hóllyhock
Iris
Lilac

20—Ivy
Maple

3—Bloom
Daffodil
Elm
Forget-me-not
Honeysuckle
Mahogany
Myrtle
Nasturtium
Orchid
Pansy
Redwood
Rose

4—Garden
Fuschia
Hemlock
Pepper
Sweet Pea

5—Carnation
Gardenia
Mignonette
Pink
Primrose

6—Chrysanthemum
Dandelion
Laurel
Lotus
Narcissus
Palm

Poplar
Rosewood
Tulip

7—Cowslip
Crocus
Fern
Flower
Geranium
Hyacinth
Marigold
Poppy
Sun-flower

8—Begonia
Blue-bell
Dahlia
Jasmine
Rhododendron
Hickory
Pine

9—Bud
Buttercup
Holly
Magnolia
Oak
Sycamore

11—Dogwood
Heart's Ease
Violet
Chestnut
Weeping-willow

22—Daisy
Lily
Cedar
Hard Maple (22-2)

IN APPRECIATION

For the splendid co-operation of others in the professional world, whose untiring research has made Vocational Guidance and the human equation matters of serious consideration in present-day affairs, we are deeply grateful.

To the many writers whose works have been an inspiration;

To our students of *Finding Yourself by Numbers*, and

To our friends in various climes who have expressed their appreciation of *Numerology Made Plain*, and are still with us, after its fifth edition, we extend our appreciation for the stimulus you have given us toward further research. We trust that CHARACTER GRAMS will prove a like stimulant to you and provide an answer to your present queries.

Whatever your question or problem may be, there are forces in life that will assist you, if you only learn to work with them. The road of least resistance is an easier one than the fighting plan. Despite the opinion of the world in general that we must fight to win, the fact remains that if we fight the law of life, it will fight back, and justly so.

In Part I, Chapter XI, we spoke of the writer's trinity of 3-6-9 as the dominant vibration in the name of The Curtis Publishing Company. If one has this influence in name or birth it does not necessarily follow that he can be a great publisher without effort. This number vibration only indicates where he can place his efforts with the least opposition to his developed talents.

The purpose of the analyst is not, how to cheat nature, or fool the public, but to assist round pegs to find their roundholes. Remember when you hear an artist sing, to give a little thought to the work that lies behind the finished effort. Unless you are willing to discipline your-self to the rules and laws of any endeavor, you are not apt to succeed.

The sign posts on the highway of life only point the direction—you must do your own walking.

Let the expression of your talent, do your talking.

"Believe in Yourself, and other people will share your opinion." No matter how steep the trail, how rugged the road, YOU ARE WORTH THE EFFORT!

> Let naught deter you from your goal
> But be the master of your soul,
> Knowing well the spoken word
> From the vibrant ether of your world
> Creates the form you hold in mind.
>
> Think not your aim can be too high,
> DESIRE. Thy goal doth prophesy,
> And nothing is impossible;
> For the Law which stands invincible,
> Returns to You, your thoughts in kind.

Griel Yvon Taylor

CHARACTER GRAMS

PLAYING COUNTERS

Tear out the perforated pages which follow.

Paste on light cardboard before cutting into individual counters.

Spell out your name as shown in examples on pages 51 and 52 in Part I, Chapter X.

Use the Single Number Counters for the Name Totals.

Follow Rules for Playing on pages 70, 71 and 77.

1	2	3	4	5	6	7	8	9
A 1	B 2	C 3	D 4	E 5	F 6	G 7	H 8	I 9
J 1	K 2	L 3	M 4	N 5	O 6	P 7	Q 8	R 9
S 1	T 2	U 3	V 4	W 5	X 6	Y 7	Z 8	& 9
1	2	3	4	5	6	7	8	9
11	22							

Cut as Needed

1	2	3	4	5	6	7	8	9
A1	B2	C3	D4	E5	F6	G7	H8	I9
J1	K2	L3	M4	N5	O6	P7	Q8	R9
S1	T2	U3	V4	W5	X6	Y7	Z8	&9
1	2	3	4	5	6	7	8	9
11	22							

Cut as Needed

1	2	3	4	5	6	7	8	9
A 1	B 2	C 3	D 4	E 5	F 6	G 7	H 8	I 9
J 1	K 2	L 3	M 4	N 5	O 6	P 7	Q 8	R 9
S 1	T 2	U 3	V 4	W 5	X 6	Y 7	Z 8	& 9
1	2	3	4	5	6	7	8	9
11	22							

Cut as Needed

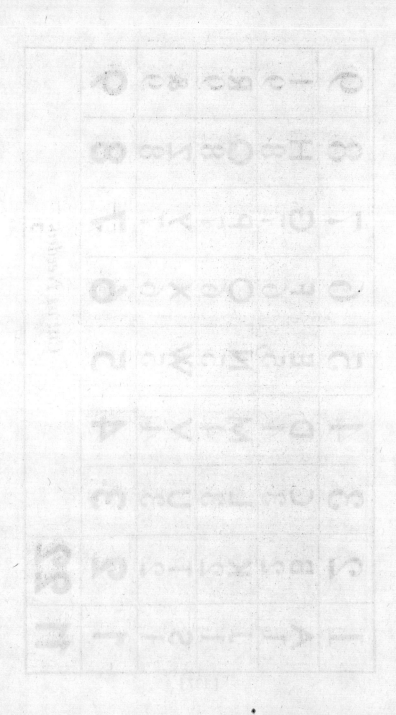

1	2	3	4	5	6	7	8	9
A 1	B 2	C 3	D 4	E 5	F 6	G 7	H 8	I 9
J 1	K 2	L 3	M 4	N 5	O 6	P 7	Q 8	R 9
S 1	T 2	U 3	V 4	W 5	X 6	Y 7	Z 8	& 9
1	2	3	4	5	6	7	8	9
11	22							

Cut as Needed

1	2	3	4	5	6	7	8	9
A1	B2	C3	D4	E5	F6	G7	H8	I9
J1	K2	L3	M4	N5	O6	P7	Q8	R9
S1	T2	U3	V4	W5	X6	Y7	Z8	&9
1	2	3	4	5	6	7	8	9
11	22							

Cut as Needed